DISCUSSION PAPER 74

FOCAC Twelve Years Later
Achievements, Challenges and the Way Forward

LI ANSHAN, LIU HAIFANG, PAN HUAQIONG,
ZENG AIPING and HE WENPING

PEKING UNIVERSITY, SCHOOL OF INTERNATIONAL STUDIES
in cooperation with
NORDISKA AFRIKAINSTITUTET, UPPSALA 2012

Indexing terms:
Africa
China
International cooperation
South south relations
Foreign policy
Institutional framework
Evaluation

Language checking: Peter Colenbrander

ISSN 1104-8417

ISBN 978-91-7106-718-0

© The authors and Nordiska Afrikainstitutet 2012

Production: Byrå4

Print on demand, Lightning Source UK Ltd.

Contents

Acronyms and Abbreviations

ADB	African Development Bank
AHRDF	African Human Resources Development Fund
AIDS	Acquired Immune Deficiency Syndrome
AU	African Union
CADF	China-Africa Development Fund
CCP	Chinese Communist Party
DRC	Democratic Republic of the Congo
ECOWAS	Economic Community of West African States
FOCAC	Forum on China-Africa Cooperation
HIPC	Heavily Indebted Poor Countries
IMF	International Monetary Fund
LDC	Least Developed Country
MDGs	Millennium Development Goals
MFA	Ministry of Foreign Affairs
MOF	Ministry of Finance
MOFCOM	Ministry of Commerce
NEPAD	New Partnership for Africa's Development
NGO	Non-Government Organization
OAU	Organization of African Unity
OECD	Organization for Economic Cooperation and Development
PRC	People's Republic of China
SADC	Southern Africa Development Community
UNDP	United Nations Development Programme
UNECA	United Nations Economic Commission for Africa
UNEP	United Nations Environment Programme
WHO	World Health Organization
WWF	World Wildlife Fund

Preface

FOCAC Ten Years Later: Achievements, Challenges and the Way Forward, is a joint project of the Centre of African Studies, Peking University, and the Nordic Africa Institute (NAI). The report is being released ahead of the 5th Ministerial Conference of the Forum on China-Africa Cooperation (FOCAC) to be held in Beijing between 19 and 20 July 2012. Since 2008, Peking University and NAI have been collaborating on joint research on evolving China-Africa relations.

This research was financially supported by the National Fund of Social Science in China, and the World Wildlife Fund (WWF-China). The research is the first attempt to evaluate the achievements of FOCAC since its inception in 2000. The authors of the report have put forward pragmatic and sensible recommendations for institutionalizing FOCAC as a permanent platform to promote China-Africa relations for several decades to come.

The research was conducted under the leadership of Professor Li Anshan of Peking University, and the team comprised professors Liu Haifang, Pan Huaqiong (Peking University), Zeng Aiping (China Institute of International Studies) and He Wenping (Chinese Academy of Social Sciences). The draft report was later revised and refocused by a team from NAI, which included Simone Noemdoe, research consultant, and Professor Fantu Cheru, the coordinator of the BRICS/IBSA-Africa project. Peter Colenbrander, NAI's external editorial contractor, provided valuable editorial assistance.

The authors of the report affirm that FOCAC plays an indispensable role in China-Africa relations and represents a new model of South-South multilateral relations. However, to ensure FOCAC's sustainability, a number of steps must be taken by Chinese and African governments to improve current institutional arrangements and decision-making processes. In particular, the report highlights the need to create mechanisms for greater civil society and private sector engagement in both China and Africa in the process of decision-making; and to increase the frequency of follow-up procedures to ensure effective implementation of agreed targets.

It is our hope that this report will stimulate lively discussion and debate among policy-makers from China and Africa, civil society organizations and the private sector. FOCAC is an important platform for policy dialogue and all stakeholders must make extra efforts to ensure its sustainability.

Professor Fantu Cheru
Senior Research Fellow & Coordinator of the BRICS/IBSA-Africa Project
The Nordic Africa Institute
Uppsala, Sweden

Introduction

The Forum on China-Africa Cooperation (FOCAC) was established in 2000. It is a multilateral platform for exchange and cooperation between China and African countries that have formal diplomatic relationships with China, and covers various aspects of politics, trade, economy, society and culture.

There have been four FOCAC ministerial conferences to date, the third coinciding with the China-Africa Summit. FOCAC ministerial conferences are held every three years, and alternate between China and an African country. The fifth ministerial conference is scheduled for 19–20 July 2012 in Beijing.

All previous FOCAC ministerial conferences and their follow-up actions have had a great impact and deepened bilateral cooperation between China and Africa. As the government of the Peoples Republic of China prepares to host the fifth ministerial conference, this report assesses the success of FOCAC in fulfilling commitments made at previous ministerial meetings, and the challenges and opportunities for institutionalizing FOCAC as a platform for promoting China-Africa relations in coming decades.

FOCAC's achievements

FOCAC represents a new cooperation model between China, the world's largest developing country, and Africa, the continent with the highest number of developing countries. Thus, this cooperation model could provide a new basis for solving global poverty.

The forum is a new and mutually beneficial cooperation model based on mutual respect among equals, and is directly related to the legitimacy of the world's current political-economic system.

Many realistic and pragmatic achievements have been recorded over the first decade of FOCAC's existence (See Annex 1).

Purpose

More than ten years have passed since the establishment of FOCAC, an event that marked an important milestone in China-Africa history and prompted tremendous responses around the world.[1] FOCAC has played a significant role and become an important institution that could influence the current history. The purpose of this project is to study FOCAC's origins, procedures, participating institutions, mechanisms, achievements, shortcomings, and sustainability.

---

1. There were 34.2 million hits after searching 'Forum on China-Africa Cooperation' on Google (7 April 2011).

Approach to Research

This research project mainly used qualitative research methods. There were four key tools: desktop study; structured interviews (in-person and telephonic); field studies; and interactive lectures.

The desktop research analyzed the existing literature and FOCAC documents between October and December 2010. FOCAC's first decade of existence has given rise to a wide range of materials, including research reports about its principles, actions, measures and mechanisms. The main purpose of this phase of investigation was to collect and analyze FOCAC's history, achievements and problems. This research was supported by the National Social Science Fund and undertaken by the Centre for African Studies at Peking University. It was expected that certain key FOCAC participants would be interviewed, including the Chinese ministries of foreign affairs and of commerce, the China Development Bank and at least two African diplomats in China and two African organizations.

In the event, the research team interviewed the relevant stakeholders in China as well as African diplomats from Nigeria, Democratic Republic of Congo, the Sudan, Zimbabwe, Tunisia and Morocco and NEPAD and AU representatives based in China. The interviews (and lectures) were mainly in Beijing. This material was complemented by several African field trips to South Africa, Ethiopia and Zambia, among others.

Respondents included officials from the Chinese and African governments[2] and from financial institutions, as well as researchers and entrepreneurs.

The project group included three scholars from Africa, who conducted most of the African diplomatic interviews. The Chinese researchers conducted the Chinese interviews and provided additional support to the field staff doing the African interviews. Chinese, English, French and Arabic were used.

---

2.   Interviewees include Ambassadors Shu Zhan, Liu Guijin, Xu Mengsui, and the ambassadors of Morocco, Tunisia and Tanzania, as well as diplomats for the Democratic Republic of Congo, Zimbabwe, Nigeria and the Sudan and the AU representative in China.

1. China-Africa Relations: Historical Overview

1.1 Four Decades of Strategic Support

(a) 1960s – 1970s

China has long offered assistance to African countries without any political conditions attached. This approach dates back to the 'Eight Principles of Foreign Economic and Technological Aid'. From 1956 to 1996, as part of its assistance to African countries, China built nearly 800 projects across the continent including farming, fisheries, textiles, energy, transport, broadcasting and communications, hydropower dams, machinery, public and civil construction, education, health, technology, handicrafts and food processing.[3]

(b) 1970s – 1980s

During the 1970s, 33 heads of African states visited China. In 1970, China began to build the Tanzania-Zambia railway, which the West had refused to build on the grounds of cost and logistical impracticality. The Chinese government took on this enormous project and completed the line in 1976. In October 1971, with the support of other developing countries, China resumed its legal seat in the United Nations. Among the 76 countries supporting and voting for China were 26 in Africa. Chairman Mao stated clearly that 'it was black African friends who carried us back in'.[4]

(c) 1980s – 1990s

The mid-1980s were regarded as 'the golden era of China-African relations since 1949'. Twenty-nine African heads of state visited China from 1982 to 1985 and Chairman Li Xiannian visited three African countries in 1986. Chinese-African economic and trade cooperation was greatly strengthened. From the 1970s to the end of the 20th century, China signed more than 6,000 labour contracts with African countries, amounting to nearly $ 10 billion in total.

China's Africa policy also changed in the early 1980s. In 1982, the 12th conference of the CCP made two strategic decisions. Henceforward, emphasis would be on the Chinese domestic economy, thereby signalling the calculated transformation of China, and also on an independent foreign policy focused on peace and development. To emphasize the importance that Beijing attached to Chinese-African relations, Premier Zhao Ziyang made a visit to Africa just

---

3. Huang Zequan, 'Fifty Years of China-African Friendly Cooperation,' Centre for African Studies, Peking University, ed. *China and Africa*, Beijing: Peking University Press, 2000, p.45.
4. Weng Ming, 'Linxing Dianjiang: Qiao first led a mission to the UN General Assembly', Fu Hao, Li Tongcheng, eds. *Jingtian Weidi:* Diplomats at the UN, Beijing: China Overseas Chinese Publishing House, 1995, p. 9.

three months after the 12th conference. During this visit he announced the four principles that would underlie economic and technological cooperation with Africa: *sincerity, equality and mutual benefit, solidarity and common development.*

By the end of 1987, the Chinese government had completed 388 projects in Africa. At the same time, China started to reform its foreign trade and foreign assistance institutions. The financial subsidy for foreign trade exports was cancelled and foreign trade enterprises also began to take responsibility for their profits and debts. This created new conditions for increased investment in Africa. Other reforms included improving assistance to projects and separating the foreign assistance agency from other foreign enterprises. It also included training in technological and management skills for Africa, thereby marking the growing diversification of foreign assistance initiatives. These changes and reforms laid a solid foundation for the rapid development of China-African trade relations.

It can also be noted that several African presidents and prime ministers and foreign minister's visited China after the 'Tiananmen incident' in 1989. China took these visits to mean that Africa considered itself a 'true friend', according to former Foreign Minister Qian Qichen. 'They remembered that China used to help them in the past, and therefore they should try their best to support China.'[5]

(d) 1990s – 2000s

The rapid development of China-Africa relations in the 1990s required a more systematic approach to maintain the initial momentum. Africa went through tough times after it suffered drastic economic decline in the 1980s, usually described as 'the lost decade'. In an arena of economic globalization, China-Africa cooperation gave rise to opportunities and challenges. After the mid-1990s, the impact of the Western-promoted multiparty democracy processes subsided, and Africa's situation got better.

During this time, Africa's political conditions stabilized, with many countries emerging from uprisings and wars. In addition, African economies started to recover and achieved 2.4 per cent growth in 1995. The number of African countries with negative economic growth indicators decreased from 14 in 1994 to three in 1995, while those with a growth rate above 6 per cent increased from two in 1994 to eight in 1995. According to ADB statistics, Africa's economic

---

5.   Qian Qichen, *Ten Episodes in China's Diplomacy,* Beijing: World Knowledge Publishing House, 2003, pp.255–7. Also see Ian Taylor, 'China's Foreign Policy towards Africa in the 1990s,' *Journal of Modern African Studies,* 36, 3 (1998), pp.446–9.

growth rate rose to 4.8 per cent, exceeding population growth for the first time and reversing the situation of income decrease on the continent.[6]

African countries continued to signal their loyalty to China when at the 53rd conference of the UN Human Rights Commission in 1997, they, together with other developing countries, opposed a Western anti-China resolution and proposed that no action against China be taken.

Between 1990 and April 1998, 53 African heads of state, 15 African prime ministers and many African senior officials visited China.[7] These visits indicated the mutual trust between China and Africa and also promoted China-Africa relations. Africa has for many years supported China over Taiwan and Tibet issues. It also supported China's candidacy for the WHO director-general's position and China's bid to host the 2008 Olympic Games.

With the 'Going Abroad' policy, China moved from ideology to pragmatism and sharpened its focus on trade and investment. The 'two resources and two markets' tactic encouraged Chinese enterprises to enter and invest in Africa. China-Africa development relations gained momentum in 1995, including visits to 23 African countries by Chinese leaders. An oil project was initiated in the Sudan and African oil became the top commodity import into China, so that trade between China and Africa increased by 48.3 per cent. Bilateral trade became the new trend and Chinese enterprises increased their African investments, while an increasing number of African businessmen participated in Chinese trade fairs.

China had supported the African anti-colonial struggle and after returning as a permanent member of the United Nations Security Council continued to uphold justice for African countries, fighting firmly against external forces attempting to interfere in their internal affairs. Africa received significant Chinese foreign aid, despite China's own poor economic situation and the difficulties it faced. In addition to industrial and agricultural projects, China supported infrastructure development, a milestone in the early period of African independence. These large projects played an important role in nation-building in these African countries.[8]

In 1996, Chairman Jiang Zemin visited six African countries and delivered his 'Build a New Historical Monument to China-African Friendship' speech at

---

6.   Xia Jisheng, 'Reviews of African Economic Development in the 1990s,' *Asian and African Studies*, 7 (1997), Beijing: Peking University Press, pp.296–9.

7.   Chen Gongyuan, *China-African Relations and the Quest of African Issues*, Beijing: Chinese Association of African Studies, 2009, p.132.

8.   It is inappropriate to over-emphasize the cost of these buildings. Instead, their political and cultural significance should be noted. Li Anshan, *Study on African Nationalism*, Beijing: China's International Broadcast Publisher, 2004, pp. 291–300. Regarding China's aid for big projects in Africa, see *Fifty Years of Sino-African Friendly Cooperation*, Beijing: World Knowledge Publishing House, 2000.

the OAU (now AU) headquarters. He put forward five principles for building durable, stable, comprehensive and cooperative China-Africa relations for the 21st century: sincere friendship; equality and mutual respect; common development and mutual benefit; consultation and cooperation in international affairs; and looking to the future to build a better world. These principles became the guiding principles in China-African cooperation in the new era.

Throughout this period, Chinese investments in Africa accelerated, rapidly increasing trade volumes. China also implemented its governmental preferential loan scheme in 1995 after a three-year trial period, and framework agreements on preferential loans were concluded with 16 African countries by the end of 1996. New forms of foreign loans were gradually accepted by recipient countries. By the end of 2000, the number of countries that had signed preferential loan framework agreements had increased to 22.

Table 1: Volume of Trade between China and Africa 1990–99 (in US$ 100 million)

Year	Volume of Trade	Africa's Exports to China	China's Exports to Africa
1990	9.35	2.75	6.60
1994	26.43	8.94	17.49
1995	39.21	14.27	24.94
1996	40.31	14.64	25.67
1997	56.71	24.64	32.07
1998	55.36	14.77	40.59
1999	64.84	23.75	41.08

Source: Almanac of China's Foreign Economy and Trade, various years. (1991: 305; 1995–96: 389 and 410; 1996–97: 554 and 579; 1997–98: 363 and 391; 1998-99: 372 and 405; 1999–00: 398 and 432; 2000: 459 and 492), China Foreign Economy and Trade Publishing House.

In order to improve understanding of China and strengthen friendship and long-term cooperation between China and African countries, the first seminar of China-Africa economic management officials took place on 3 August 1998. Twenty-two officials from 12 African countries took part. Proposed by former Chinese President Jiang Zemin, these seminars were to be held twice a year. Another layer to this partnership is the Chinese-driven communications and exchanges on culture, education and health with Africans.[9] These rapid changes in China-Africa relations and cooperation necessitated further institutionalization.

---

9.   Editorial Group of Educational Cooperation and Communication between China and Africa, *Educational Cooperation and Communication between China and Africa*, pp. 3–5; Drew Thompson, 'China's Soft Power in Africa: From the 'Beijing Consensus' to Health Diplomacy,' China Brief, 5:21 (13 October 2003), pp.1–4.

2. Forum on China Africa Cooperation (FOCAC)

Economic globalization, the progress made by Western countries in the post-Cold war period in expanding their economic engagement with Africa, provided an incentive for China to take a proactive decision to develop a comprehensive approach to engaging the African continent. African senior officials realized the importance of a China-Africa cooperation mechanism and proposed the establishment of FOCAC. Chinese academics and political professionals advised on upgrading and institutionalizing China-Africa relations and these ideas were finally put into practice. Without the active participation of and promotion by the African side, the establishment of FOCAC would have been impossible.

2.1 The First Decade of FOCAC

There is a sense of continuity in the history of China-Africa interaction within a partnership framework explicitly underpinned by development, equality of treatment between the parties and respect for sovereignty. China-Africa relations fluctuated before the establishment of FOCAC, but generally speaking, they have been marked by cooperation and mutual support on the international stage.

2.2 New Opportunities and Challenges

Pushed by economic globalization, the pace of 'going abroad' by Chinese enterprises accelerated. 'Going outside' was not only a matter of business behaviour, but was directed and supported by the country's foreign policy.

This is indicated by various Chinese state visits to Africa to promote Chinese trade. Vice Premier Zhu Rongji announced in 1995 on his African visit that to support joint ventures by Chinese and African enterprises and to provide initial funding, China would provide preferential government loans. When Premier Li Peng visited Africa in 1995 and 1997, he stated that 'the Chinese government encourages Chinese enterprises to have direct cooperation with African enterprises, and supports Chinese companies in investing in Africa to enlarge the fields of cooperation.' Chairman Jiang Zemin stated in 1996 on his trip to Africa that 'the Chinese government encourages mutual cooperation, broadening trade, increasing African imports, and finally promoting the balanced and fast development of China-African trade'.[10]

Africa's political and economic improvement, the West's adjustment of its Africa policy and the opportunities and challenges provided by economic globalization contributed to the establishment of FOCAC.

---

10. Huang Zequan, 'Fifty Years,' p.49.

From 1996 to 2004, the Chinese Foreign Ministry authorized the China Foreign Affairs University to host nine workshops (in French and English) for African diplomats to improve their understanding of China. Some African leaders and envoys to China (including Ethiopia and Mauritius) proposed establishing a 'one to multi-partnership', but China did not initially think this practicable. Attending diplomats from Mauritius, Benin and Madagascar were already proposing the establishment of a relevant mechanism between China and African countries, but this was not put into practice.

2.3 Origins of FOCAC

The common perception is that FOCAC was initiated by the Chinese government.[11] Some even argue it was part of a 'grand strategy'.[12] As a matter of fact, the most important push for the establishment of FOCAC was by Africans. The new situation required fresh measures and innovative institutions, an increasing number of African countries proposed establishing a new kind of partnership with China.

How to face the new challenges and protect their legitimate interests were the common questions China and African countries were contemplating at the turn of the century. Some African nations even argued that China-Africa relations should adjust to the new situation by building large-scale high-level contact mechanisms in the manner of the US-Africa Business Forum, the Commonwealth Conference, the Franco-African Summit, the Tokyo International Conference of African Development and the Euro-African Summit, as well as strengthening bilateral communications on issues of mutual concern such as peace and development.[13]

In February 1998, the then ambassador to Zimbabwe returned to China and became head of the Department of African Affairs in the Ministry of Foreign Affairs. In March 1998, the newly appointed foreign minister visited Guinea, Côte d'Ivoire, Ghana, Togo and Benin. During this visit, he realized the im-

---

11. Ann Cristina Alves, 'Chinese Economic Diplomacy in Africa: The Lusophone Strategy,' Chris Alden, Daniel Large and Ricardo Soares de Oliveira, eds., *China Enters Africa: A Rising Power and a Continent Embrace*, London: Hurst, 2008, p.72; Mwesiga Baregu, 'The Three Faces of the Dragon: Tanzania-China Relations in Historical Perspective,'Kweku Ampiah and Sanusha Naidu, eds., *Crouching Tiger, Hidden Dragon? Africa and China*, Scottsville: University of KwaZulu-Natal Press, 2008, p.163.

12. Helmut Asche, 'China's Engagement in Africa: A Survey,' paper presented at international conference 'China in Africa: Who Benefits? Interdisciplinary Perspectives on China's Involvement in Africa, 'Johann Wolfgang Goethe University, Frankfurt am Main Germany, 14-15 December 2007.

13. Yao Guimei, 'FOCAC and its influence on China-African Economic Cooperation,' Chen Gongyuan, ed., *A Probe into the New Strategic Partnership between China and Africa*, Beijing: Chinese Association of African Studies, 2007, p.263.

portance of Africa on the international political and economic stage and the urgency of reinforcing China-Africa cooperation.

In 1999, Madagascar's minister of foreign affairs, Lila Ratsifandrihama, visited China. During this visit, she expressed a strong pro-China position and called for greater cooperation between China and Africa. She continued: 'Since the bilateral relations between China and African countries are strong and considered to be in such good condition as both sides continue to cooperate in many areas, why not consider establishing a multilateral forum?'[14] At this time, the US, France and Japan were adjusting their African policies.

At the beginning of the new millennium, with its new challenges and opportunities, China realised that China-Africa cooperation could be raised to a new level. The initiatives, particularly by Madagascar, as well as the push from within the Department of African Affairs in the Chinese Ministry of Foreign Affairs, led to the setting up of a process to formalize China-Africa relations. Though the proposal that emerged was not initially considered as viable, the proponents believed it represented an opportunity to even resolve outstanding bilateral issues. Eventually, after several rounds of discussion, the proposal was submitted to the State Council. Chairman Jiang Zemin and Premier Zhu Rongji immediately ratified the proposal.[15]

China's own sensitivity over Western competition in Africa and the urgency of building a permanent cooperation mechanism prompted the Chinese government to accept the African suggestion to establish FOCAC.

Table 2: The History of FOCAC Conferences

First Ministerial Conference

Date	12–14 October 2000
Place	Beijing, China
Participants	China, 44 African countries, 17 organizations
Papers Issued	*Beijing Declaration of FOCAC; Guideline of China-Africa Cooperation in Economic and Social Development*
Commitments	• Promote political cooperation, create a favourable environment for China-Africa business affiliation and trade; • Provide assistance to African countries; • Give preference to import African products; • Establish China-Africa Joint Business Council and China- Africa Products Exhibition Centre to promote bilateral trade and to facilitate access for African products to the Chinese market; • Provide special funds to support well-established Chinese enterprises to invest in African countries; • Cancel RMB10 billion in HIPC and LDC debts ; • Send extra medical teams to African countries;

---

14. Tang Jiaxuan, *Jingyu Xufeng*, Beijing: World Knowledge Publishing House, 2009, p.433.
15. An interview with Ambassador Liu Guijin, 30 December 2010, Beijing.

- Grant more scholarships to African students to study in China and send teachers to Africa;
- Set up communications between African and Chinese universities and establish an African Human Resources Development Fund.
- Cooperate in environmental management.

Second Ministerial Conference

Date   15–16 December 2003
Place   Addis Ababa, Ethiopia
Participants China, 44 African countries, AU etc.
Papers Issued *FOCAC – Addis Ababa Action Plan (2004–06)*
Commitments
- Enhance cooperation in the development of human resources, train 10,000 African personnel;
- Open up market and grant free tariff access for some commodities from the LDCs in Africa;
- Expand tourism cooperation with Africa, name eight African countries for Chinese tourist groups that cover their own travel expenses;
- Sponsor the 'Meeting in Beijing';
- Increase people-to-people exchanges with Africa and hold China- Africa Youth Festival.

Beijing Summit and Third Ministerial Conference

Date   4–5 November 2006
Place   Beijing, China
Participants China, 48 African countries, AU, etc.
Papers Issued *Declaration of the Beijing Summit of FOCAC; FOCAC – Beijing Action Plan (2007–09)*
Commitments
- Double the 2006 assistance to Africa by 2009;
- Provide $ 3 billion of preferential loans and $ 2 billion of preferential buyer's credits;
- Set up CADF, the funding to reach $ 5 billion to encourage Chinese companies to invest in Africa and support them;
- Build an AU conference centre;
- Cancel debts owed by HIPCs that matured at the end of 2005;
- Increase the number of export items from 190 to over 440, offer zero-tariff treatment to the 30 African LDCs;
- Establish 3-5 trade and economic cooperation zones;
- Train 15,000 African professionals; send 100 senior agricultural experts to Africa. Set up 10 special agricultural centres;
- Build 30 hospitals, provide artemisinin (anti-malaria drug) to the value of RMB300 million, build 30 malaria prevention and treatment centres in Africa;
- Dispatch youth volunteers;
- Build 100 rural schools in Africa and increase Chinese scholarships for African students from 2,000 per year to 4,000 per year by 2009.

Fourth Ministerial Conference

Date	8–9 November 2009
Place	Sharm el-Sheikh, Egypt
Participants	China, 49 African countries, AU, etc.
Papers issued	*Declaration of Sharm el-Sheikh of FOCAC; FOCAC – Sharm el-Sheikh Action Plan (2010–12)*

- Establish a China-Africa partnership to respond to climate change, build 100 clean energy projects for Africa;
- Enhance cooperation with Africa in science and technology. Launch a China-Africa science and technology partnership, carry out 100 joint scientific and technological research demonstration projects, and accept 100 African postdoctoral fellows to conduct scientific research in China;
- Provide $ 10 billion concessional loans to African countries; set up a $ 1 billion special loan for small and medium African businesses;
- Cancel debts associated with interest-free government loans due to mature by the end of 2009;
- Give zero-tariff treatment to 95% of products from African LDCs;
- Increase Chinese-built agricultural technology demonstration centres in Africa to 20, send 50 agricultural technology teams to Africa to train 2,000 African agricultural technicians;
- Provide medical equipment and anti-malaria equipment worth RMB500 million to hospitals and malaria prevention and treatment centres and train 3,000 doctors and nurses for Africa;
- Build 50 China-Africa friendship schools and train 1,500 school principals and teachers; increase Chinese scholarships to Africa to 5,500 by 2012;
- Launch a China-Africa joint research and exchange program.

Source: The website of Ministry of Foreign Affairs, the People's Republic of China: http://www.focac.org/eng/

3. FOCAC Members and Their Functions

FOCAC is a multilateral cooperation institution involving multilevel inter-actions between China and African countries through various exchange and communication channels. There are 27 member agencies in China involved in FOCAC policy-making and implementation, both of which are continually ad-justed according to the situation. Africa has more than four levels of institutions participating in policy-making and implementation.

3.1 Chinese Members and Their Functions

The Chinese **Follow-up Action Committee of FOCAC** (see Chart 1) spans a wide range of departments, including major ministries, administrative bu-reaux, government offices and financial institutions. The three core ministries are Foreign Affairs, Commerce and Finance, which are responsible for executing FOCAC policies according to its mandate.

The Ministry of Foreign Affairs is in charge of diplomatic policy on Afri-can issues, as well as overall FOCAC policies. Chinese embassies and consulates in Africa have the important role of maintaining contact with related African ministries and understanding their expectations and demands. They are respon-sible for providing feedback to the relevant Chinese ministries, which in turn make draft proposals within their respective spheres of responsibility.

Trade, investment, assistance and training within FOCAC are the responsi-bility of the **Ministry of Commerce**. This ministry also takes care of commu-nications between the Chinese Economic and Commercial Counsellor's Office in Africa and African governments. It also plays an important role in planning and implementing economic and aid projects, including facilitating public bid-ding by Chinese companies on aid projects, making policy to support Chinese companies in enhancing trade and investment in Africa, and taking charge of aid projects, such as building schools, hospitals, anti-malaria centres and agri-cultural demonstration centres and training African professionals.[16]

The **Ministry of Finance** is critical in offering financial support to China-Africa cooperation within FOCAC, including budget approval and supervision.

FOCAC's Follow-up Action Committee is led by the Chinese State Council and operates according to the Chinese national system. It is an open forum, and other Chinese government departments or organizations may in future join as and when required.

---

16. Interview with Wang Cheng'an, former general-direction of the Department of Aid to Foreign Countries, secretary-general of the Forum for Economic and Trade Cooperation between China and Portuguese-speaking Countries, 27 December 2010, Peking Univer-sity.

Chart 1: FOCAC Structure

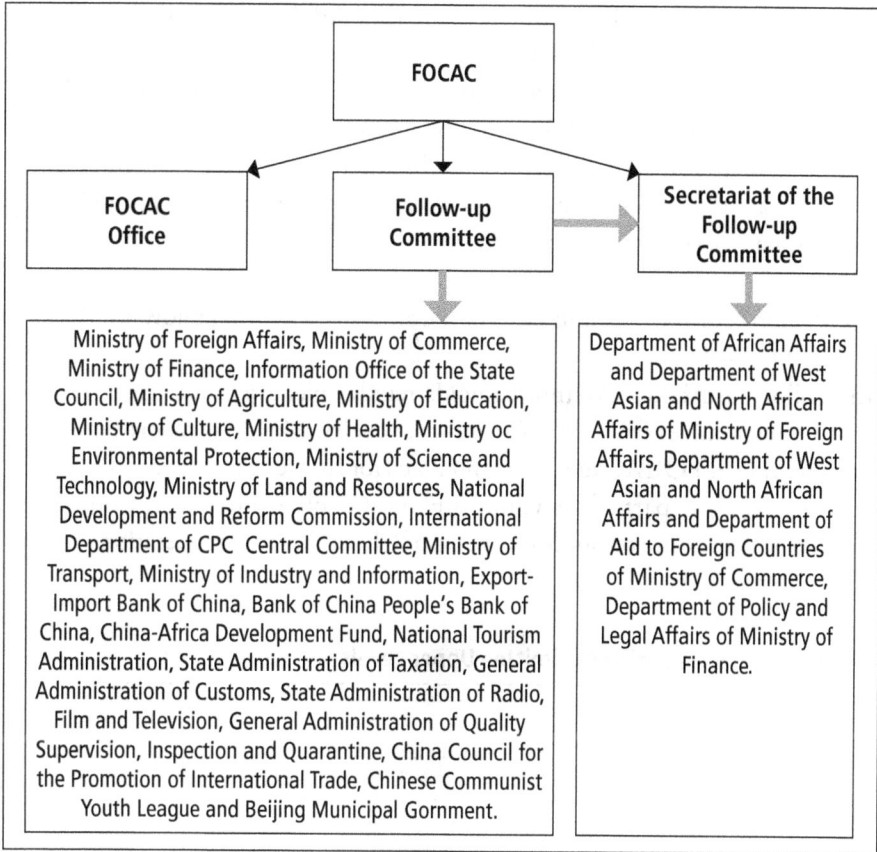

FOCAC

FOCAC Office	Follow-up Committee	Secretariat of the Follow-up Committee
Ministry of Foreign Affairs, Ministry of Commerce, Ministry of Finance, Information Office of the State Council, Ministry of Agriculture, Ministry of Education, Ministry of Culture, Ministry of Health, Ministry oc Environmental Protection, Ministry of Science and Technology, Ministry of Land and Resources, National Development and Reform Commission, International Department of CPC Central Committee, Ministry of Transport, Ministry of Industry and Information, Export-Import Bank of China, Bank of China People's Bank of China, China-Africa Development Fund, National Tourism Administration, State Administration of Taxation, General Administration of Customs, State Administration of Radio, Film and Television, General Administration of Quality Supervision, Inspection and Quarantine, China Council for the Promotion of International Trade, Chinese Communist Youth League and Beijing Municipal Gornment.		Department of African Affairs and Department of West Asian and North African Affairs of Ministry of Foreign Affairs, Department of West Asian and North African Affairs and Department of Aid to Foreign Countries of Ministry of Commerce, Department of Policy and Legal Affairs of Ministry of Finance.

3.2 Chinese Follow-Up Action Committee Leadership

The Chinese Follow-up Action Committee of FOCAC operates has **two alternating** chairs and is administered through **a secretariat of the Follow-up Action Committee.** The two chairmen are the vice-ministers of African Affairs in the Ministry of Foreign Affairs and in the Ministry of Commerce. The current (2012) serving chairs are Zhai Jun, vice-minister of foreign affairs, and Fu Ziying, vice-minister in the Ministry of Commerce.

The Follow-up Action Committee secretariat comprises five departments:
• Department of African Affairs;
• Department of West Asian and North African Affairs in the Ministry of Foreign Affairs;
• Department of West Asian and North African Affairs;
• Department of Aid to Foreign Countries in the Ministry of Commerce; and
• Department of Policy and Legal Affairs in the Ministry of Finance.

Currently, the secretary general of the Follow-up Action Committee is the director-general of the Department of African Affairs. The Follow-up Action Committee Secretariat holds regular meetings with core members and with the participation of other departments and leading ministries, such as the Policy Planning Department of Ministry of Foreign Affairs.

The secretariat is responsible for coordinating the 27 Chinese members, but does not have the authority to decide and enforce policies and has limited ability to coordinate between major ministries.

3.3 Plenary Conference and Enlarged Conference of the Follow-up Action Committee

The Follow-up Action Committee holds regular plenary conferences with invited representatives from the 27 member agencies. Members report on the implementation of FOCAC measures and plans for future conferences.[17] Organizations not officially part of the Chinese FOCAC Follow-up Action Committee, but able to contribute on specific aspects of China-African cooperation, are also invited to participate.

Chart 2: Follow-up Action Committee Upper Levels

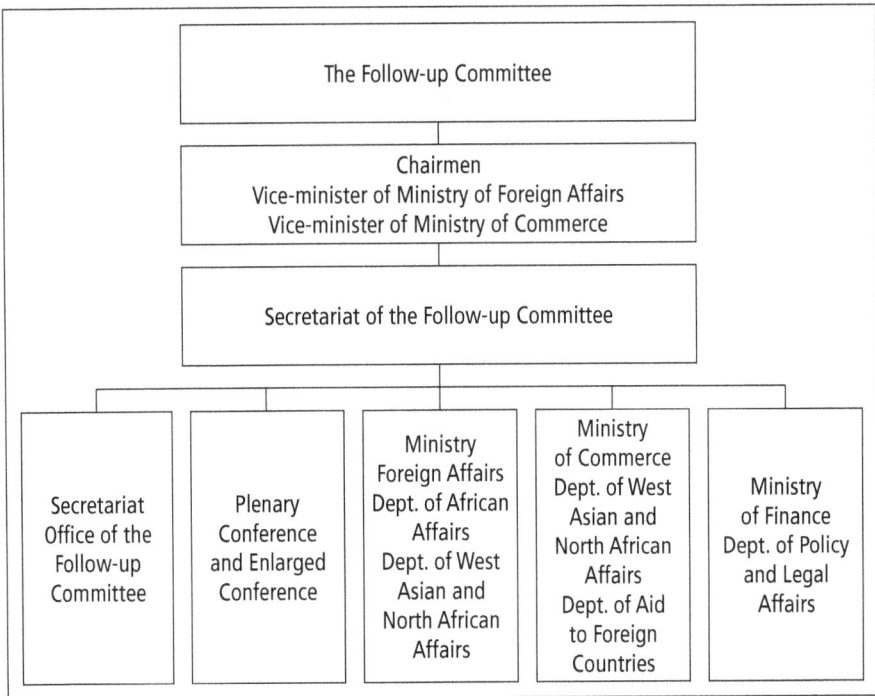

The Follow-up Committee				
Chairmen Vice-minister of Ministry of Foreign Affairs Vice-minister of Ministry of Commerce				
Secretariat of the Follow-up Committee				
Secretariat Office of the Follow-up Committee	Plenary Conference and Enlarged Conference	Ministry Foreign Affairs Dept. of African Affairs Dept. of West Asian and North African Affairs	Ministry of Commerce Dept. of West Asian and North African Affairs Dept. of Aid to Foreign Countries	Ministry of Finance Dept. of Policy and Legal Affairs

---

17. Interview with Shu Zhan, former Chinese ambassador in Eritrea, 5 November 2010, Peking University.

3.4 Participating Chinese Government Departments

This overview provides insight into the scope and depth of China's engagement with FOCAC. It also provides an update of the general progress in each area of cooperation.

(a) Education

The Ministry of Education is in charge of China-Africa educational cooperation, including providing government scholarships for African students, training professionals and providing human resource development support. The ministry held a China-Africa education ministers' forum, a FOCAC sub-forum on education, in 2005. It initiated the China-Africa Universities 20+20 Cooperation Plan, which linked 20 Chinese universities with 20 African counterparts to conduct research and jointly train students.[18] The Department of International Cooperation and Exchange is the executive body.

(b) Science and Technology

Science and technology cooperation is the responsibility of the Ministry of Science. The Department of International Cooperation has hosted one round table conference on China-Africa science and technology cooperation. The ministry has initiated a China-Africa Science and Technology Partnership Plan. According to this plan, China will support 100 joint research and demonstration projects, invite 100 African postdoctoral candidates to conduct scientific research in China and offer research equipment to all African scientific researchers on their return home.

(c) Agriculture

Agricultural cooperation is undertaken by the Ministry of Agriculture. China has complementary cooperation potential in this field with most African countries, which are still bedevilled by an underdeveloped agricultural sector and food insecurity, while China feeds some 22 per cent of the world population from just 7 per cent of arable land. China's experience with agricultural technology offers Africa options for resolving its food crisis and safeguarding food security. The Department of International Cooperation is responsible for sending senior experts to Africa to teach agricultural technology. The ministry, along the Fourth Bureau (African Affairs) of the International Department of CCP Central Committee also jointly hosted the first China-Africa agricultural cooperation forum.[19]

---

18. 'Launching ceremony of 20–20 plan held in Guangzhou',
     http://www.gov.cn/gzdt/2010-06/02/content_1619271.htm, 2 June 2010.

19. Wang Huihui, '中非农业合作论坛在北京开幕',
     http://www.moa.gov.cn/ztzl/zfnyhzlt/ltdt/201008/t20100812_1616251.htm, 12 august 2010.

(d) Health

The Ministry of Health leads China-Africa health and medical cooperation and assistance. China has been sending medical teams to Africa since 1963, thereby making a great contribution to the continents' medical and health conditions. The ministry invites groups of African health officials to China to enhance understanding, trust and exchanges between China and African countries. The Department of International Cooperation is the executive body under the FOCAC framework.

(e) Culture

Leading the cultural and communication exchanges with Africa is the Ministry of Culture. It has organized visits by Chinese artistic troupes to Africa and has hosted the 'Meeting in Beijing' international arts festival and African culture in focus programmes in different Chinese cities. The Bureau for External Cultural Relations is the executive body. Other institutions, such as the State Administration of Radio, Film and Television, also take part in China-Africa cultural exchanges and cooperation.

(f) Environment

The Ministry of Environmental Protection is in charge of cooperation in this field between China and Africa, as well as promoting bilateral sustainable development with an economic and social focus. The China Environmental Protection Foundation, affiliated to the ministry, hosted the 'China's Environmental Protection towards Africa' initiative in 2003. The ministry co-hosted with UNEP the China-Africa environmental protection conference in Kenya in 2005. In 2006, the ministry participated in the African ministerial conference on the environment in Congo (Brazzaville) and established the UNEP China-Africa Environment Centre.[20] In that year, the ministry also hosted a water pollution and water management seminar for African environmental protection officials.[21]

In 2009, at the fourth FOCAC ministerial conference, China proposed the establishment of a China-Africa partnership to address climate change and hold senior official consultations on an occasional basis. These events contributed to the strengthening of cooperation in several fields, such as satellite weather monitoring, development and utilization of new energy, combating desertification and environmental protection in urban areas.

---

20. '祝光耀在非洲国家环境部长会议上倡议　推进中非环境合作多样化', http://www.cenews.com.cn/historynews/06_07/200712/ t20071229_26905.html, 26 May 2006.

21. '国际司领导出席'非洲国家水污染和水资源管理研修班'开幕式', http://gjs.mep.gov.cn/qyhjhz/200601/t20060111_73295.htm, 11 January 2006.

(g) Inter-party Communication

Inter-party communication between China and African countries is led and handled by the International Department of the CCP Central Committee. The department sometimes organizes activities with other ministries, for instance, the first China-Africa agricultural cooperation forum was co-hosted with the Ministry of Agriculture. The Fourth Bureau (African Affairs) is the executive body.

(h) Mass Media

The Information Office of the State Council and State Administration of Radio, Film and Television are in charge of press and media cooperation between China and Africa. Recently, these two institutions have strengthened this cooperation. They also enhanced Chinese media influence in Africa to challenge false international media reports about China-Africa cooperation, and issue news reports reflecting China's and Africa's perspectives.

The Information Office and Ministry of Foreign Affairs held a joint FOCAC news conference on 15 July 2009 with information officials, mainstream media organisations, African news agencies in China and other representatives from 27 African countries. They discussed the media's role in China-African relations and how to improve the right of developing countries to speak in the international media.[22] China's main media agencies, Xinhua News Agency, China Radio International and Central China TV, have increased the number of stations in Africa following the establishment of FOCAC, and have active exchanges with local mainstream media. African media personnel visited China to attend training programmes offered by the administration. The Administration of the Information Office, Department of International Cooperation and Training is the executive body.

(i) Youth Development

The Chinese Communist Youth League manages youth exchange activities between China and Africa with the object of increasing mutual understanding among young people. In order to deepen Chinese-African friendship and mutual understanding, the Youth League selects qualified Chinese volunteers to go to Africa for a period of service. Moreover, the Youth League organizes the China-Africa youth festival. The Department of International Liaison, the Department of Youth Volunteers and the China Youth Federation are the executive bodies.

---

22. '中非合作论坛——新闻研讨会举行',
   http://media.people.com.cn/GB/9661775.html, 15 July 2009.

(j) Transport

The Ministry of Transport is in charge of China-African transport cooperation, which is focused on shipping and aviation. Under the FOCAC framework, the Administration of Maritime Affairs and the International Marine Organization jointly offer seminars to train presidents of African marine universities and African maritime commissioners. These seminars have helped improve maritime management and promote China-Africa maritime cooperation. In the field of aviation, the Chinese government encourages greater cooperation and the opening up of direct air routes between China and Africa, which will benefit personal contact and goods transportation.

By the end of 2009, China had signed civil aviation agreements with 15 African countries.[23] Airlines from Egypt, Ethiopia, Zimbabwe, Kenya and Algeria have launched regular direct services to China, while China has initiated direct air services from Beijing to Lagos, Luanda and Khartoum. From 2008 to 2011, in an effort to improve civil aviation safety in African countries, the National Civil Aviation Administration of China promised an annual contribution of $ 100,000 to the comprehensive regional implementation plan of the International Civil Aviation Organization for aviation safety in Africa.[24]

(k) Mining

Chinese-African cooperation on geological prospecting, mineral resources and energy is the responsibility of the Ministry of Land and Resources. The China Geological Survey, affiliated to the ministry, hosted seminars on mineral resources management and technicians for African officials and technicians in an effort to strengthen China-Africa geological cooperation and exchange. The ministry hosted the African energy and mineral resources seminar' in Beijing on 30 November 2010, at which the current status of and prospects for China-African cooperation in energy and mineral resources was discussed.[25]

(l) Tourism

China's national tourism administration is dedicated to promoting China-Africa tourism cooperation and the signing of tourism cooperation memorandums or tourist destination agreements with African counterparts. The Department of Tourism Promotion and International Liaison is the executive body. By the end of 2009, mainland Chinese had visited 28 African tourism destinations.

---

23. *2010 Report on China-Africa Economic and Trade Relations,* Chinese Academy of International Trade and Economic Cooperation, p.13.
24. *2010 Report on China-Africa Economic and Trade Relations,* Chinese Academy of International Trade and Economic Cooperation, p.14.
25. 2010 非洲能源矿产研讨会在京举行', http://www.mlr.gov.cn/xwdt/jrxw/201012/t20101206_799639.htm, 6 December 2010.

3.5 Vehicles to Promote Trade, Commerce, Banking and Investment

China has developed a number of trade, commerce and banking institutions and mechanisms to govern its growing relations with Africa. These use existing and developing infrastructure to increase the effectiveness of FOCAC as a vehicle for implementing bilateral and multilateral cooperation.

(a) The **China Council for the Promotion of International Trade (CCPIT)** is dedicated to promoting cooperation between Chinese and African entrepreneurs. The China-Africa business forum is a FOCAC sub-forum convened by the CCPIT during ministerial conferences to stimulate pragmatic bilateral cooperation. The Department of International Liaison of the council is the executive body. Under the leadership of CCPIT, the China-Africa joint chamber facilitated activities to improve mutual cooperation. The chamber also established a liaison office in Wuhan.

(b) The National Development and Reform Commission creates an advantageous environment for Chinese enterprises entering Africa. They support the establishment of inter-government investment cooperation institutions between China and African countries and promote Chinese-African economic and technological cooperation. The Foreign Investment Department is the executive body.

In addition, the commission is also engaged in tariff exemptions for exports from LDCs in Africa. Also, the commission, Ministry of Finance, Ministry of Commerce and General Administration of Customs have established a tariff exemption group to decide a number of issues, including the list of tariff exemption commodities, rules of origin and the implementation periods.

(c) Information Technology cooperation is the responsibility of the **Ministry of Industry and Information**. It drives industrial cooperation and encourages collaboration between Chinese and African medium and small enterprises.

(d) Promoting Chinese-African trade development under the FOCAC framework is the responsibility of the General Administration of Customs. Together with the Ministry of Commerce, Ministry of Finance and National Development and Reform Commission, the administration makes decisions on issues such as preferential tariff and tariff exemption policy towards LDCs in Africa.

(e) The **State Administration of Taxation** signs tax agreements with African states that benefit Chinese-African tax cooperation and promote economic and trade cooperation. An example is the signing of the Convention for the Avoidance of Double Taxation and the Prevention of Fiscal Evasion with Respect to Taxes on Income between China and Ethiopia on 14 May 2009. This was the first tax agreement between China and an African country after the Beijing Summit.

(f) Inspection and quarantine matters in China-Africa cooperation and exchange are the responsibility of the **General Administration of Quality Supervision, Inspection and Quarantine**. It is responsible for strengthening cooperation in product-quality supervision and inspection so as to smooth the development of China-African economic exchanges and serve China's overall diplomacy towards Africa.

Under the FOCAC framework, the administration has signed quality-control cooperation agreements with Sierra Leone, Kenya, Ethiopia, Algeria, Egypt and Burundi, for the inspection of Chinese exports to Africa before shipment and is in discussion with other African countries about similar agreements. The administration also hosts supervision, inspection and quarantine training seminars for African officials.

(g) The **People's Bank of China** is dedicated to promoting China-Africa financial cooperation. The bank participates in the African Multilateral Development Bank in order to deepen China-Africa cooperation. It hosted the China-African high-level seminar on economic reform and development strategies in 2003, the 2007 annual meetings of the board of governors of the African Development Bank group, and the seminar on development and financial support for small and medium enterprises in 2010. The International Department is the contact and executive body.[26]

(h) The **Export-Import Bank of China (Ex-Im Bank)** is the Chinese government's bank responsible for international cooperation, specifically supporting enterprises' imports and exports, contracts for foreign construction projects and investment abroad. Through business, mixed and buyers' credits and preferential loans, Ex-Im Bank plays a crucial role in promoting African economic and social development. The process of preferential loan aid be-

---

26. Huang Peizhao '中非经济改革与发展战略高级研讨会召开', http://news.sina.com.cn/o/2003-10-17/2259938897s.shtml,17 October 2003; Lin Junhui, '中小企 业发展与金融支持研修班'在宁举行', http://www.js.xinhuanet.com/xin_wen_zhong_xin/2010-11/23/content_21460388.htm, 23 November 2010.

gins when companies explore projects, and is followed by the bank's evaluation and an inter-governmental framework agreement. The International Department is the executive body. It has a representative office in Southeast Africa.

(i) The **China-Africa Development Fund** is one of eight measures announced at the Beijing Summit and third ministerial conference. It is both a private equity fund and a direct equity investment fund, and supports cooperation between Chinese enterprises and African countries as well as the implementation of China-Africa economic and trade cooperation zones. The fund's first-phase financing goal is $ 1 billion, 40 per cent of which is directly funded by the Chinese government. Its final disbursement goal is $ 5 billion. The fund is invested in a wide range of fields in order to strengthen African economic ability. Most of these projects are newly established, covering agriculture, manufacture and infrastructures. The fund is operated on market-oriented principles.[27]

(j) The **Bank of China** is the most internationally oriented state-owned commercial bank in China. It supports Chinese enterprises in developing Africa and enhances cooperation with local banks in Africa. It also supports the development of local enterprises and the achievement of mutual benefit and win-win outcomes in China-Africa cooperation. Branches are located in Zambia and South Africa, and they offer good social and economic benefits.

(k) Issuing special loans for small and medium enterprises in Africa in accordance with one of the eight measures (see Annex 1, Table 1) announced by Premier Wen Jiabao at the fourth FOCAC summit is the responsibility of the **China Development Bank**. The bank has already issued special loans to such enterprises in Egypt, Ethiopia and Kenya.

(l) The **State Administration of Industry and Commerce** collaborates with the General Administration of Quality Supervision, Inspection and Quarantine on quality control. Its market department also cooperates with the Department of Trade in the service of the Ministry of Commerce and the Department of Policy and Legal Affairs of the General Administration of Customs.

---

27. Interview with Shi Yongjie, Senior Executive Director of Office of the Advisory Committee, Research and Development Department, China-Africa Development Fund, 24 December 2010.

3.6 Other Relevant Chinese Institutions

In addition, other Chinese institutions participate in the follow-up actions announced at FOCAC ministerial conferences, though they are not official members of the Follow-up Action Committee.

(a) Acting as a city for national to international coordination, the **Beijing municipal government** is in charge of guaranteeing social order, security and logistics during FOCAC conferences hosted there. It is required to mobilize citizens to coordinate the conference, control traffic and take security measures. Moreover, the Beijing municipal government promotes China-Africa cooperation in political, economic, social and cultural fields.

(b) The **Chinese People's Association for Friendship with Foreign Countries** and the Follow-up Action Committee jointly held a China-Africa NGO exchange conference on 24 July 2009 in Beijing. It was intended to promote NGO cooperation between China and Africa. The **All-China Women's Federation, the China Council for the Promotion of International Trade**, the **Chinese People's Institute of Foreign Affairs**, as well as the **China Federation of Youth** and other organizations were invited to the conference.

(c) The **Chinese-African People's Friendship Association (CAPFA)**, affiliated with the Chinese People's Association for Friendship with Foreign Countries, appealed to Chinese ophthalmologists to provide medical services in Africa.[28] CAPFA also started the China-Africa Friendship Award in 2006 to celebrate Chinese and African personnel and groups with an outstanding history of promoting China-Africa friendship. Among the awards have been those for the 10 Chinese who deeply moved the African people, the five African people who deeply moved the Chinese people and the top 10 Chinese enterprises in Africa.[29]

(d) The **Chinese Law Society** hosted the FOCAC law forum on two occasions with the second forum taking place in Beijing on 16 September 2010. The objective is to promote China-Africa law and legal cooperation.

(e) Technological cooperation on surveying and mapping is driven by the **State Bureau of Surveying and Mapping**. It hosted the China-Africa surveying

---

28. Li Chunguang, Suo Qiang, 'Chinese ophthalmologist went to Africa to serve cataract patients, ',http://www.cnr.cn/09zth/gmx/xgbd/201103/t20110318_507806570.html, 18 March 2011.

29. http://english.cri.cn/other/movingafrica/index.htm

and mapping cooperation conference in Tanzania on 22 April 2010. During this conference, the possibilities for China-African cooperation in this area were explored with a view to promoting mutually beneficial common development.

China-Africa cooperation activities cover a many fields, almost all of which can be included under the FOCAC framework.

3.7 African Members and Their Function(s)

Unlike the highly unified and centralized structure of the Chinese side, the relevant African FOCAC institutions are varied: multilateral and bilateral, centralized and decentralized. These characteristics reflect the essential features of China-Africa relations, with one country on one side and one continent with 53 countries on the other. Generally speaking, many African countries operate on several levels in relation to FOCAC, with each level serving different functions.

Chart 3: Structure of FOCAC on the African Side

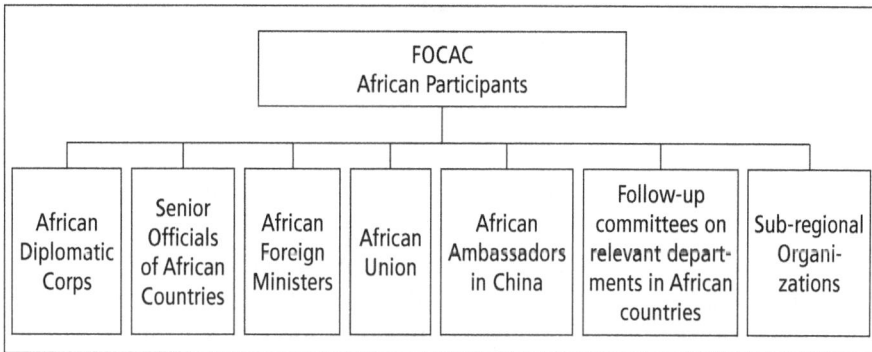

FOCAC African Participants						
African Diplomatic Corps	Senior Officials of African Countries	African Foreign Ministers	African Union	African Ambassadors in China	Follow-up committees on relevant departments in African countries	Sub-regional Organizations

(a) African Diplomatic Corps

The African diplomatic corps meets with China's Follow-up Action Committee every three months (or at least twice a year) to discuss specific issues, and it holds a special conference as required. In turn, China's Follow-up Action Committee reports to the African diplomatic corps on the latest developments in China-Africa cooperation and the implementation of FOCAC measures. The committee will also listen to the advice, suggestions and demands of the African participants on how to further China-Africa relations, especially FOCAC. The Chinese Follow-up Action Committee raises and presents ideas to the African diplomats and includes summaries of their responses in a revised set of ideas. A new report is sent to the diplomats, who in turn start a consultative process with the relevant departments in their home countries.

Chart 4: The African Diplomatic Corps Process

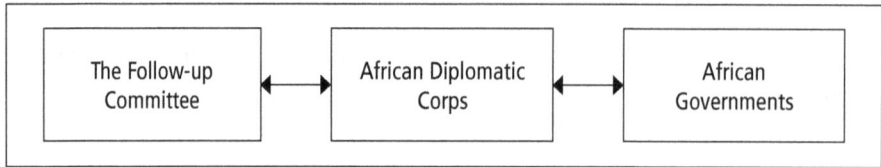

The Follow-up Committee	←→	African Diplomatic Corps	←→	African Governments

For example, this communication and cooperation channel played an important role in the preparations for the fourth FOCAC ministerial conference in Egypt in November 2009. The secretariat of the Follow-up Action Committee consulted with African diplomats in Beijing to exchange views on the preparations for the conference and the implementation of the eight measures emerging from the Beijing Summit. Officials from the ministries of foreign affairs, commerce and finance, as well as African diplomats from 45 countries, participated in the consultation. Another follow-up action committee created by the African ambassadors in China coordinated with African countries about organizing FOCAC meetings.[30]

(b) Senior Officials of African Countries

The Chinese-African Senior Office Meeting (SOM) is convened one year before the next ministerial conference to discuss follow-up activities from the last ministerial conference. It also meets a few days before the upcoming ministerial conference to complete the preparations. The SOM, like the ministerial conference, is held alternately in China and Africa, with meetings being chaired by China and the host as co-chair.

Ministers of foreign affairs and the ministers of international cooperation and/or financial and economic affairs participate in the ministerial conference.

The SOM comprises directors-general or those of equivalent rank from the counterpart departments of the participating countries. Over 200 representatives from China and 46 African countries as well as six African regional organizations met in Beijing from 21 to 23 August 2005 to prepare for the November 2006 FOCAC Beijing Summit. They formulated inputs and gave advice to deepen China-African cooperation.[31]

Marking the 50th anniversary of the inauguration of diplomatic relations between New China and African countries, FOCAC was upgraded from a ministerial conference to a summit in 2006. A special SOM to prepare for the summit was held on 1–2 November 2006 in Beijing, with participants from China and 48 African countries.

---

30. Interview with a Sudanese diplomat, 2 December 2010, Sudanese embassy in China.
31. '中非合作论坛第四届高官会在北京开幕',
    http://www.chinanews.com/news/2005/2005-08-22/26/615004.shtml, 22 August 2005.

(c) **African Foreign Ministers**

In a move to strengthen the institutional mechanisms, Chinese and Africa leaders agreed during the Beijing Summit to set up a system of regular political dialogue between foreign ministers. Specifically, they agreed to hold political consultations in New York on the sidelines of the UN General Assembly in the first year after each summit. On 26 September 2007, the first such China-Africa foreign ministers' political consultation took place during the UN General Assembly session to exchange views on major issues of common interest.

The next session took place in China and Chinese officials, African ambassadors and African government delegates spent two days discussing and consulting on issues such as climate change and the MDGs, and reached agreement on joint Chinese-African measures to respond to these challenges.[32]

(d) **African Union**

The African Union, as a FOCAC member, also has a role in coordinating African participants. A senior official serves as the forum coordinator and facilitates AU discussions on China's ideas before every FOCAC conference. In addition, Chinese ambassadors to Africa seek advice from African countries to guarantee smooth communications in the forum and to gather feedback.

At the moment, NEPAD serves as AU's technical section by making substantial suggestions and transforming political will into concrete agenda. An AU official has realized that the African side lacks the capacity to make full use of FOCAC resources. He hoped for more opportunities to collaborate with Chinese scholars, including conducting joint research on FOCAC, making suggestions to both sides, supervising FOCAC, and publishing research relevant to African embassies and departments and supportive of Africa's preparations in its cooperation with China. At the same time, researchers should give advice to the Chinese government in order to resolve common problems.[33]

(e) **Other Relevant African Institutions**

Three additional channels are relevant to communications with China under the FOCAC framework: African ambassadors in China, follow-up action committees or relevant departments in African countries and African sub-regional organizations.

Currently most FOCAC projects are implemented at **country level,** with individual ambassadors to China playing a critical role.

Currently, only South Africa and Ethiopia have follow-up institutions. In

---

32. Interview with a diplomat from DRC, December 2010, DRC Embassy in China.
33. Interview with Fantahun H. Michael, AU senior official and FOCAC projects coordinator, 21 September 2009, AU headquarters.

these instances, **national follow-up action committees** or national government departments help to implement agreements.

Other countries coordinate their interactions with FOCAC through the **Asia and Pacific department** of their ministries of foreign affairs. If FOCAC projects require involvement by other ministries, the ministries of foreign affairs will make contact with them. According to a Zimbabwean embassy official in China:

> FOCAC focuses on various sectors of the [African] economy. In Zimbabwe, we have got a focal point in every sector of our national economy, for instance, in agriculture, health and education. All of these are coordinated by the Ministry of Foreign Affairs which acts as a spokesman in foreign relations. As such it liaises with the Zimbabwean Embassy in Beijing and the Chinese Embassy in Harare, through which, Zimbabwe coordinates its programme within the FOCAC.[34]

The DRC, for example, has a secretariat in the presidential office in charge of monitoring the contracts the country has signed with Chinese state-owned companies. It is called the Coordination and Follow-Up Bureau of the Sino-Congolese Partnership Programme. It is directed by an executive secretary, Moise Ekanga.[35] Thus, different countries have different institutions in charge of coordination and cooperation.

(f) Regional Organ Coordination

China has stressed the importance of inviting African sub-regional organizations to workshops in China since the start of this collaboration programme between itself and Africa. From 1999 to 2003, at the request of the Chinese Ministry of Foreign Affairs, the China Foreign Affairs University hosted nine seminars in English and French for participants from African sub-regional institutions on understanding modern China. This strategy promoted relations between China and sub-regional bodies as well as creating a platform for economic cooperation.[36]

---

34. Interview with Zimbabwean diplomat in China, December 2010, Zimbabwean embassy.
35. Interview with a diplomat from DRC, December 2010, DRC embassy in China.
36. Li Anshan, 'On the Adjustment and Transformation of China's African Policy,' *West Asia and Africa*, 8 (2006), pp.11–20.

4. FOCAC Operating Mechanisms

FOCAC is the result of a common endeavour: a multi-level interaction between China and Africa from the preparatory stages to its formal launch and entry into operation. The dynamic creativeness of both sides, for instance in joint promotion, has been equally important.

4.1 Preparations and Formation

Earlier in this report, we gave an overview of this process, which produced two basic documents, the Beijing Declaration and the Economic and Social Development Programme. These started a consultative process.[37] FOCAC is the product of the interaction between China and Africa during the preparation and formation process.

On the one hand, FOCAC is clearly not a product of China's one-sided efforts to lay out its strategy, as many rumours suggested. On the other, although the original idea for FOCAC can be attributed to Africa, the long-term friendly relations between China and Africa served as the foundation for establishing a permanent cooperation mechanism at the end of the 1990s. Thus, both sides could reach agreement. The process was also characterized by a series of multilevel interactions, as the diagram below shows.

The first is the core level of direct interaction between heads of the Chinese and African states.

The second level is the SOM, a face-to-face exchange between Chinese and African officials (above and below the level of director-general). This mechanism made a big contribution to the finalization of basic documents and to the immediate institutionalization of FOCAC. As a result, SOM was institutionalized as part of FOCAC's multi-level interactions, resulting in SOM meetings being held between any two FOCAC sessions to monitor the implementation of measures and to prepare for the next ministerial conference.

The third and most permanent level is the interaction between Chinese and African diplomats and the host countries at all possible levels. For instance, after the State Council ratified the proposal to establish FOCAC, the Chinese ambassador to Guinea contacted the host government and tabled the possibility of setting up a forum between China and African countries.[38]

4.2 Africa's Contribution to the Preparations for and Formation of FOCAC

Three main contributions to the preparations for and formation of FOCAC were made by the African side. First, it helped to raise original ideas; second, it

---

37. Interview with Amb. Liu Guijin, 31 December 2010, Beijing.
38. Interview with Amb. Xu Mengshui, 22 December 2010, Beijing.

Diagram 1: FOCAC's Multi-level Interaction Mechanism

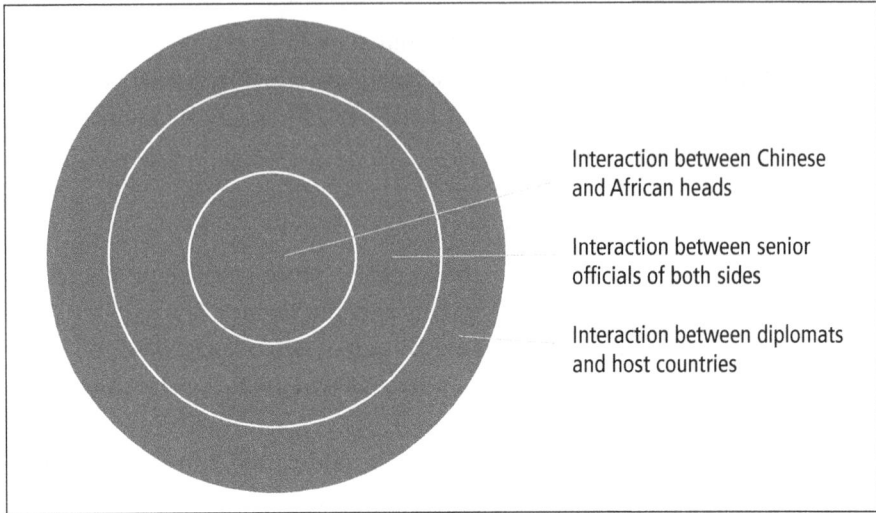

Interaction between Chinese and African heads

Interaction between senior officials of both sides

Interaction between diplomats and host countries

enriched the two basic FOCAC documents; and third, it pushed for FOCAC's immediate institutionalization.

The pace of FOCAC's implementation and institutionalization was different in China and Africa. While the Chinese opted for gradual institutional development through SOM over the course of two years before making a final decision, African states opted for speeding up the process and pushed for immediate establishment.

Once agreed, the process of FOCAC's formation was based on a consensus that would become characteristic of the forum itself. The contrast in behaviour and mindset between the China and Africa reflects the former as prudent and moderate and the latter as passionate and straightforward. These differences have been recognized and appreciated by officials in the Chinese Ministry of Foreign Affairs.[39]

4.3 Characteristics of Chinese Decision-making

In creating FOCAC, China's used both top-down and bottom-up approaches. This could be interpreted as a manifestation of traditional democratic centralism and the multilayered decision-making mechanisms that have guided China's foreign affairs strategies since the 1980s.

Chinese foreign policy actors are diversified, but play joint roles. In the FOCAC preparation process, China shared the same view as Mauritius, but did not propose the idea to the State Council immediately. Instead, it decided that the

---

39. Interview with Amb. Liu Guijin, 31 December 2010, Beijing.

Department of African Affairs convene a plenary meeting to discuss the feasibility of the idea. During the first meeting, departmental officials were divided on the idea. Consequently, more investigations and meetings followed until consensus was reached on the founding of FOCAC. Discussions were also held at other levels, for instance with all Chinese diplomats worldwide (held once every four years) and with diplomats accredited to Africa (held once a year), in order to have all foreign affairs personnel give their opinions and suggestions.[40]

Once these processes were completed, a formal proposal was written by the Ministry of Foreign Affairs and then submitted to the State Council.

4.4 Constant Improvement: Process of Policy-Making

Since its institutionalization, FOCAC's operations are carried out in accordance with the basic principles and models outlined during its formation. At the same time it invites new members with more practical experience and the field of cooperation is expanded.

For example, Malawi joined FOCAC after establishing formal ties with China in 2008; the AU, which used to be an observer, finally joined by the end of 2010. In addition, besides the 26 government ministries, the Chinese Follow-up Action Committee accepted the Beijing Municipality as its 27th member because of the capital's role in hosting the FOCAC Summit in 2006.

The issues of interest to FOCAC decision-makers have become more diverse and comprehensive. For instance, at the third meeting in 2006, sociocultural cooperation was discussed at the same level as political and economic cooperation. The trend was accentuated during the fourth conference in 2009. Eight new measures were proposed, including measures regarding clean energy, to replace the 'eight old measures' from 2006. This update exemplified the new priorities in FOCAC's mission and agenda, which now included long-term sustainability and people's livelihoods.

This new content demonstrated fresh commitment and the need for new working methods and characteristics, including transparency, a scientific approach to and institutionalization of decision-making. The effective and efficient fulfilment of all these commitments necessitated scientific feasibility studies and outstanding organizational skills. Moreover, if all these projects are to be accepted and monitored, comprehensive communication and exchanges with local communities are required. This process is far from perfect, yet it is on the right track.

---

40. Interview with Amb. Liu Guijin, 31 December 2010, Beijing.

4.5 FOCAC: A platform for Mutual Learning and Decision-making

FOCAC is characterized by equal interaction at multiple levels and mutual respect. An undeniable fact is that although FOCAC was institutionalized at its first ministerial conference, to date there has not been an organization established to articulate, represent and coordinate African members' objectives. So far, only South Africa and Ethiopia have set up follow-up organizations to coordinate with the Chinese. All the other members still rely for coordination with China on their embassies in Beijing and their ministries of foreign affairs or of international cooperation.

The Chinese Follow-up Action Committee was established in 2001. It is responsible for ongoing coordination with the African diplomatic corps (especially the heads of the African diplomatic corps and of sub-regions). This committee of FOCAC holds meetings with the African diplomatic corps every two or three months. The current decision-making procedure within FOCAC mainly stems from this kind of interaction (as illustrated in Diagram 2). The Chinese side plays the main role in taking initiatives and meeting commitments, including convening meetings and collecting opinions and suggestions from members. Below is a brief diagram to illustrate the current decision-making procedure:

(a) Principle First, Planning Second: The Choice of Projects

This procedure can also be attributed to China's economic strength. Assistance from the Chinese government to African countries has been given since bilateral

Diagram 2: Current decision-making procedure

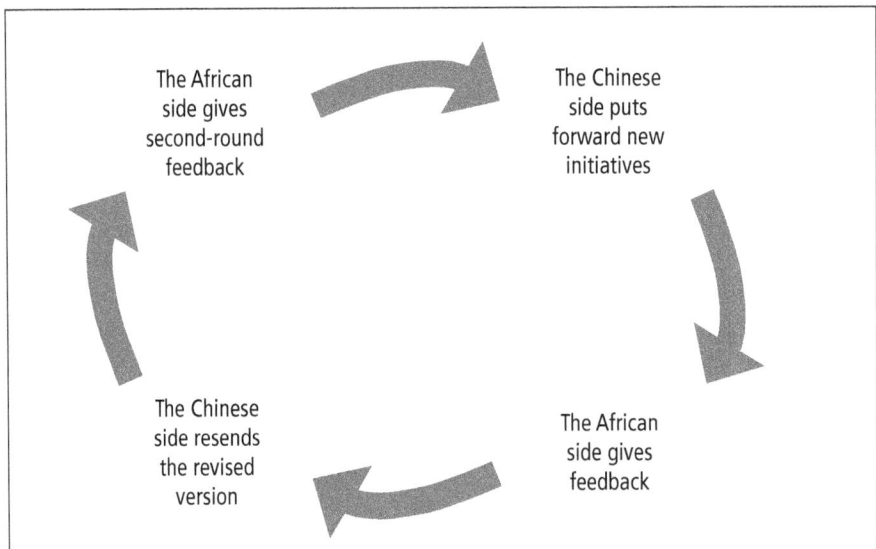

Diagram 3: Intersecting Multi-level Interactions

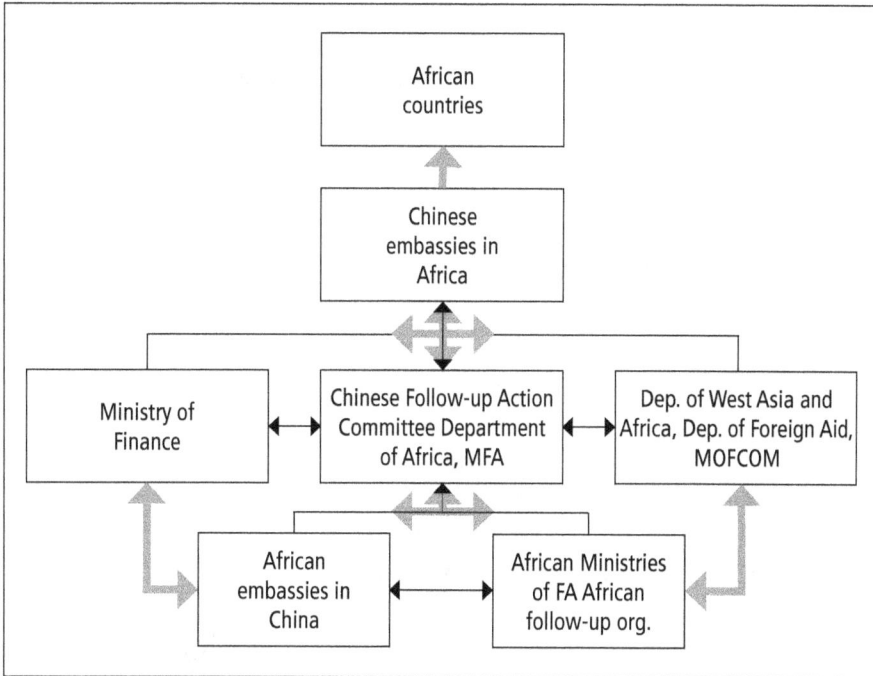

```
                    ┌─────────────────┐
                    │    African      │
                    │   countries     │
                    └─────────────────┘
                             ▲
                    ┌─────────────────┐
                    │    Chinese      │
                    │  embassies in   │
                    │     Africa      │
                    └─────────────────┘
                          ◄═══►
┌──────────────┐   ┌──────────────────────┐   ┌────────────────────────┐
│  Ministry of │◄─►│ Chinese Follow-up Action│◄─►│ Dep. of West Asia and │
│   Finance    │   │  Committee Department  │   │Africa, Dep. of Foreign Aid,│
│              │   │    of Africa, MFA      │   │        MOFCOM          │
└──────────────┘   └──────────────────────┘   └────────────────────────┘
                          ◄═══►
      ┌──────────────┐         ┌──────────────────┐
      │   African    │◄───────►│ African Ministries│
      │ embassies in │         │   of FA African   │
      │    China     │         │   follow-up org.  │
      └──────────────┘         └──────────────────┘
```

relations were first established, and is still increasing in terms of both scope and geographical reach.[41]

A China-driven FOCAC will eventually be able to integrate both traditional diplomatic channels and FOCAC's multi-dimensional mechanisms of assistance to Africa. In fact, all the relevant Chinese ministries in charge of aid are now included in the Chinese Follow-up Action Committee.

(b) Intersecting Multi-level Interactions in the Decision-making Process

Since its entry into operation, the FOCAC decision-making process has embodied the characteristics that were identified and accepted during the preparation and formation phase.

As shown in Diagram 3, the Chinese Follow-up Action Committee secretariat has regular meetings and discussions with the African diplomatic corps as the first level of contact. Communication between Chinese embassies and host countries constitutes another level. Furthermore, both Chinese and African diplomats report to their respective governments or ministries. Coordination among the 27 member units of the Chinese Follow-up Action Committee represents another sub-level. Although Chinese ambassadors and the economic and

---

41. Zhou Hong, '60 years' foreign aid of China: Reviews and Prospects,' *Waijiao Pinglun*, 5 (2010), pp. 3–11.

trade consuls have relatively low decision-making authority, they work closely with local African communities (and local civil societies) that could influence the committee on the projects to be chosen. Therefore, communications between Chinese embassies and the Chinese Follow-up Action Committee could be regarded as the third level.

The Department of Africa of the Ministry of Foreign Affairs has acted as the secretariat of the Follow-up Action Committee, along with the Department of West Asia and Africa under the Ministry of Commerce. Together they take on the core role of coordinating both the Chinese and African embassies, drafting and submitting reports to the Ministry of Finance in order to apply for disbursements, etc. Although the Ministry of Finance does not participate directly in the decision–making process, it makes the final decision on which projects will be supported, based on the proposals from the Ministry of Foreign Affairs and Ministry of Commerce. Therefore, these three ministries are regarded as the core organizations of decision-making mechanism.

(c) Roles of Chinese and African Embassies

As mentioned above, both Chinese and African embassies play a very important role in bilateral relations, but the Chinese embassies generally play a bigger role in the decision-making process. This led to questions by some Chinese organizations, which expressed doubts about whether African diplomats contacted their own capitals. This doubt arose during the preparations for and formation of FOCAC, when the Chinese realized that in-country officials often expressed different opinions from diplomats to China.[42] Certain Chinese organizations also distributed questionnaires to African embassies to elicit the opinions and suggestions of African countries regarding Chinese assistance projects. However, the survey results were barely satisfactory.[43]

By contrast, the Chinese diplomats, who were often selected from the Ministry of Foreign Affairs and the Ministry of Commerce (some directly from the Department of Foreign Aid), were efficient and responsible. They carried out basic feasibility studies of all economic cooperation and aid issues. In the process of planning, formulating and fulfilling all commitments under FOCAC, the Chinese diplomats played an appropriate role.

Nevertheless, Chinese diplomats also differ in their personal characteristics, visions, capacities, working modes and ability to deal with host countries. Although the common aim of the units in the Follow-up Action Committee is promoting bilateral cooperation, almost all the members have different interests and objectives.

---

42. Personal Interview, 31 December 2010, Beijing.
43. Personal Interview, 15 March 2011, Beijing.

The differences are attributable to the decentralization and diversification that now underlies decision-making in Chinese foreign policy. As some scholars have recently suggested, it is time to openly discuss these differences in order to make policy-making more rational and scientific.[44] The same could be true of FOCAC's decision-making.

(d) Scientific Approaches to Decision-making
The strategy to apply a more scientific approach to FOCAC decision-making is gradually unfolding. The most important principle is respect for African wishes by giving African partners two to three opportunities for making inputs before the two sides jointly discuss and investigate the feasibility and implementation of proposals at multiple levels. Furthermore, FOCAC will gradually include other international organizations, international standards on human rights, labour rights, environmental protection, and so forth, which will eventually give the assurance of the objectivity of the scientific decision-making process.

One notable example is Ex-Im Bank. Since the introduction of concessional loans in 1995, Ex-Im Bank has requested the feasibility reports about environmental issues from Chinese companies (the requests came before the publication of the Equatorial Principle). Since 2004, Ex-Im Bank has requested a separate report about the potential environmental impact of any company applying for funding. Learning from the Merowe Dam experience, Ex-Im Bank has decided to send delegations to do a feasibility study and a follow-up evaluation regarding the impact of the project on both the environment and local communities.[45]

(e) Adjusting to Circumstances
All the above characteristics show that FOCAC policy-makers have been trying as best they can to adapt to each period's specific circumstances and were constantly adjusting their opinions.

For instance, after the formal launch of FOCAC, the Chinese Follow-up Action Committee continued to maintain contact with the African diplomatic corps and sustained liaison with African governments and relevant ministries. This approach indicated an initial lack of experience in the Chinese Follow-up Action Committee, which at the FOCAC preparation stage was reliant on the Department of Africa operating under the Ministry of Foreign Affairs and still lacked the experience to deal with multilateral international mechanisms. Thus it worked on the premise that direct contact with the African diplomatic corps

44. Wang Yizhou, 'Some reflections on the Chinese foreign policy analysis,' *Waijiao Pinglun*, 4 (2010), pp.8–13.
45. Interview with Zhao Changhui, 15 December 2010, Beijing.

was a communications shortcut, but it soon learned that this approach did not necessarily yield the expected 'one voice' response.

This experience taught the Chinese that African diplomats do not always represent the ideas, views and vision of their home countries. Although they understood the situation in China, since they live in Beijing, this does not necessarily mean their home officials share this understanding. The committee thus decided to readjust its approach to maintain extensive and multi-level communications. This is another example of 'crossing the river by groping for stones', and shows how FOCAC is constantly changing and improving its working processes.

5. Evaluation of FOCAC

In the first decade of its existence, FOCAC focused primarily on promoting China-Africa relations. China could use it as a platform and effective instrument to engage in collective dialogue, exchange experiences about governance, enhance mutual trust and continue practical cooperation with African countries.

5.1 FOCAC Achievements

As FOCAC becomes increasingly diversified and its involvement in various fields more comprehensive, its international influence is also growing. Some specific achievements have already been outlined and will not be repeated here. Other of FOCAC's achievements in the economic, social and environmental fields will be summarized in terms of the three tenets of sustainable development.

5.2 Cooperation in Economic Development

Bilateral economic and trade cooperation has been further enhanced and has flourished following FOCAC's institutionalization. Trade, investment, infrastructure and capacity building have been comprehensively promoted. Finance, tourism and cooperation in other fields have also been gradually expanded. FOCAC, therefore, has a multi-level, extensive structure and is now at a new historical point.

5.3 Problems and Challenges

FOCAC has achieved great success in expanding and deepening cooperation in its first 10 years of operation. This study also found some problems that need to be addressed.

(a) Chinese Participation Mechanism

There are gaps in and between the Chinese participating institutions due to the absence of a coordinating body under the State Council. Currently, the Ministry of Foreign Affairs is unable to take on this role alone. Part of the problem may be that most officials from other participating institutions responsible for FOCAC are on temporary or part-time assignment, which hinders them in the whole-hearted fulfilment of their duties.

China and Africa have cooperated in many areas such as industry, agriculture, law, commerce, mining, healthcare, education, media and so on in the first decade. In some areas, sub-forums have been set up. These include the China-Africa agricultural cooperation forum under the auspices of the International Department of CCP and the Ministry of Agriculture; the China-African education ministers' forum organized by the Ministry of Education; the China-Africa legal forum by the China Law Society; the China-Africa cultural forum; the China-Africa technology forum, as well as the China-Africa joint research and exchange programmes hosted by Ministry of Foreign Affairs; and the '20 +20 Plan' under the Ministry of Education. Others include the China-Africa youth festival, China-Africa culture in focus and the China-Africa technology partner programmes.

The enthusiasm to establish the sub-forums and activities is encouraging, but they should be organized under the leadership of FOCAC and set up in some controllable manner according to a plan and agreed priorities. Rushing into mass action should be avoided. Specific sub-forums should be managed by relevant ministries instead of by multiple heads. What is more, the sub-forums are only meaningful if they have a positive response from and involvement by the African partners.

(b) African Initiatives

The enthusiasm of the AU and African regional organizations should be further encouraged. An African diplomat has noted:

> FOCAC currently has limited roles in the process of African integration. The integration of Africa is one of the main tasks of the African countries. Thus, FOCAC can make further contributions to this process only if the African countries are willing to authorize the discussion of relevant agendas about African integration in the forum.[46]

Furthermore, FOCAC is presently directed by China. Although it respects the interests of African countries in the decision-making process and follows the principle of equal consultation, there are still many proposals and policies that are made on the basis of one-sided Chinese enthusiasm. Consequently, they do not rest on a foundation of diversity born of multiple channels and angles.

Under the current FOCAC framework, participating African countries take fewer actions, mainly the result of the huge differences among the member countries and regions. This situation highlights the internal coordination problem among African countries. Many African countries have not agreed on the role the AU should play in FOCAC, a matter that has piqued the interest of many African scholars.[47]

---

46. Interviews with the representative of African Union in China. Beijing, March 2011. He pointed out that the building of the AU conference centre is the only evidence of the benefit that FOCAC has brought to African integration.

47. Francis Ikome, 'The role and place of the African Union in the emerging China-Africa partnership,'Axel Harneit-Sievers, Stephen Marks and Sanusha Naidu, eds., *Chinese and African Perspectives on China in Africa*, Oxford: Pambazuka Press, 2010, pp. 208–11.

(c) Weakness of China's Foreign Assistance

China has constantly increased the scale and intensity of its foreign assistance. However, there needs to be a coherent and unified management process. Coordination among ministries, the people's right to be informed, scientific project verification, assessment of completed projects, transparency of assistance and reinforcement of international cooperation – all of these become more challenging.

In terms of professionalism, function and scale, coordinating all these tasks is way beyond the capacity of the Ministry of Commerce. Because of the lack of unified coordination and professional management, various problems have arisen in assistance projects.

(d) To Strengthen the Role of the Professionals

At present, various professionals and experts participate in FOCAC at a lower level, including scholars, technical staff and officials. The medical field, technology, agriculture, environmental protection, law and other areas require specialized knowledge. There is room for improvement in enabling experts to play an effective role in FOCAC. For example, the Ministry of Environmental Protection is responsible for training staff and exchanging experiences regarding foreign assistance and investment projects. Although some experts have been invited to take part in the assessments, there is a lack of direct involvement by the ministry. Even as far as training is concerned, timely funding is often not in place. This challenge ought to be addressed.[48] This is definitely due to the limited capacity of the ministry, whose internal affairs absorb its energies at this stage.

We can summarize the following points:

First, FOCAC is the main inter-governmental mechanism for comprehensive China-Africa cooperation in various fields. It serves as a model of South-South cooperation based on equality and mutual benefit, and has contributed greatly to the improvement of China-African relationships in the past 10 years and enjoys great international influence.

Second, FOCAC initially paid attention to economic and social development, but without a specific development programme. The eight measures proposed at the Beijing Summit and the further eight measures proposed at the fourth ministerial conference indicate that FOCAC's programme has become more specific and that its emphasis is not only on economic and trade cooperation and development aid, but also on people's livelihoods, the environment and communications between think tanks. These changes reflect the shared understandings and practical approach of Chinese and African leaders. Moreover,

---

48. Interview with Ambassador Xu Mengshui, 22 December 2011, Beijing.

including environmental protection in the programme as part of economic and social development underscores the sustainable basis of China-Africa cooperation.

Third, with the scope of China-Africa cooperation widening and deepening, the support of civil society for China-Africa cooperation is constantly growing. In future, FOCAC should (1) improve overall planning and coordination between governmental sectors and (2) there should be a higher level of exchange between civil society in China and in Africa. In this way, FOCAC could promote cooperation between government and civil society in China-Africa relations.

Fourth, as environmental awareness grows, the field of environmental cooperation will surely grow. Environmental factors have become a common concern of decision-makers, investors and project implementers, and facilitating coordination and cooperation among them will help to guarantee sustainable development as part of China-Africa cooperation. This issue will also become a key one for FOCAC.

6. Sustainability and FOCAC: Directions for Improvement

In this chapter, FOCAC is examined from the perspective of sustainable development. It is noted that the concrete projects announced at FOCAC conferences are still in the preparation, experimental and implementation phase, so an overall assessment is premature. The social impact of FOCAC will manifest itself as its mechanisms evolve and progress is made in project implementation. Based on FOCAC's current mechanisms and practices, we make the following suggestions for improvement.

6.1 Proposed FOCAC Institutionalization Process

FOCAC could benefit from the establishment of an inter-ministerial coordinating committee led by one of China's vice premiers. The current staff within the secretariat of FOCAC's Follow-up Action Committee could serve as individual experts in order to make FOCAC more professional and scientific.

Revisiting the three-year time-frame of ministerial conferences would eliminate some limitations in the existing mechanism. Preparing and implementing a major project every three years, including agenda design and general coordination, is very difficult. Two alternatives are suggested:

(i)   Extend regional cooperation projects to six years, thereby allowing them to be discussed and considered at two ministerial conferences; or

(ii) The ministerial conference can be put on a five-year cycle, both as a result of and to promote mutual trust and cooperation in FOCAC.

Implementation of the forum's tasks must comply with the principle of unified coordination and clearly indicated responsibilities.

The mechanisms of the forum need to be opened up further in order to motivate all interested groups. FOCAC should seek to attract participation by civil society organizations in both Africa and China and give them the opportunity to play a role under its framework. The success of the recent 'Africa Brightness Action' initiative shows that Chinese NGOs can play a greater role in China-Africa cooperation in the fields of sanitation, education and poverty reduction. China could learn much from the Tokyo International Conference on African Development about encouraging intellectuals, the press, environmental organizations and other associations to engage in cooperation.

6.2 Possible Changes to Dialogue Mechanisms

Currently, the procedures illustrated in Diagram 3 above are not sufficient for capturing the increasingly rich, diverse and multi-level development issues that FOCAC will face. Several notable elements and characteristics may enable changes in future operations and processes.

Diagram 4: Potential Directions for Decision-making Processes (1)

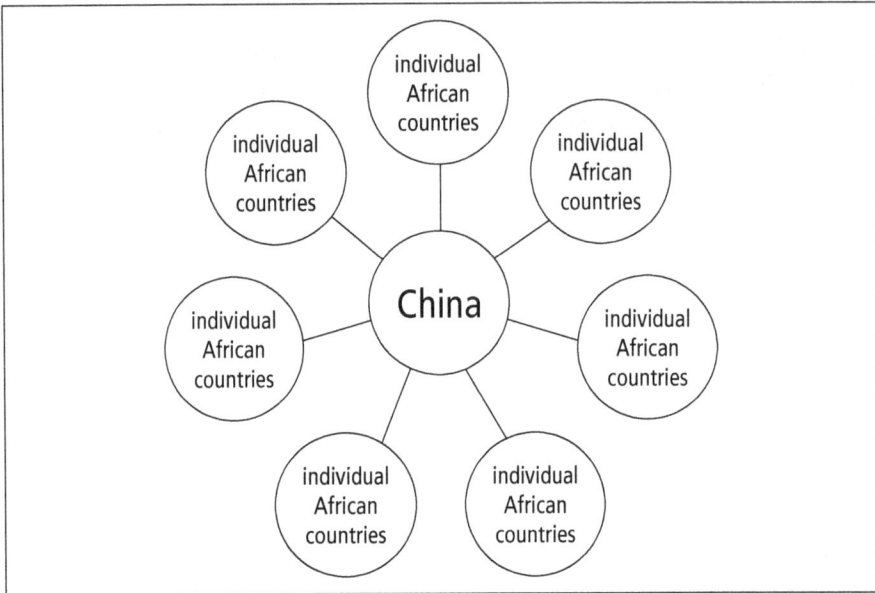

(a) Collective Ownership

The first is building on the collective dialogue mechanism and learning from Africa's deep and strong sense of ownership during the preparations for and founding of FOCAC. Africa also displayed a much more active spirit at the fourth conference of 2009, when South Africa took the initiative to propose the sponsoring of the follow-up meeting after the next FOCAC conference. This idea will be discussed by all members at FOCAC's conference in 2012.

Diagram 4 presents a possible future decision-making model.

In this model, China would be an equal participant together with any African member state or regional organization (such as the AU) at new sessions of the ministerial conference. It could also discuss and decide on new issues or proposals raised by FOCAC members on an equal footing.

African participants in FOCAC have shown their sense of ownership in many other ways. For instance, more and more African actors are extensively involved in FOCAC's decision-making process. While the China-African women's forum, the first sub-forum under FOCAC, was initiated and pushed by the Chinese side,[49] the legal forum, the second sub-forum under FOCAC, was absolutely the result of African efforts. When the African side came up with this idea, the unprepared Chinese side appeared to be perplexed.[50]

---

49. Interview with Long Jiangwen, former Minister of International Department of National Woman Association, 29 December 2009, Beijing.

50. Hong Yonghong, 'Sustainability of FOCAC: Reflections on investment in Africa from a legal perspective,' speech given on 28 February 2011, School of International Studies, Beijing University.

Diagram 5: Potential Directions for Decision-making Processes (2)

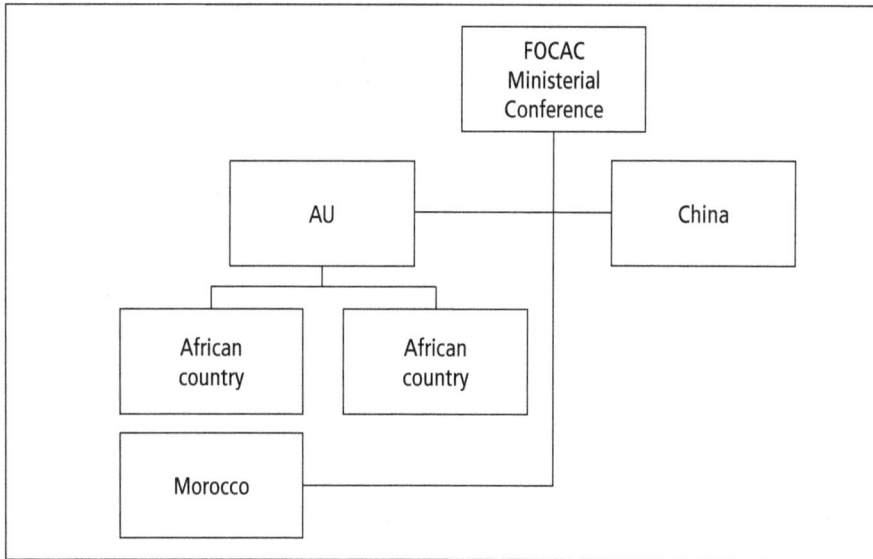

(b) Inclusive Participation

The inclusion of the AU as a full member of FOCAC at the end of 2010 reinforced the position and function of this regional body and joint mechanism for regional and sub-regional organizations. The AU now has a greater possibility of becoming the umbrella organization that would directly coordinate matters with China on behalf of African countries. This trend, however, does not exclude the possibility that non-AU members, such as Morocco, will continue to have direct contact with China, as illustrated in Diagram 5.

Diagram 6 proposes an option whereby China could eventually coordinate FOCAC activities with only regional or sub-regional organizations (in theory, representing each member state):

6.3 FOCAC and Sustainability

The secretariat of the Follow-up Committee of FOCAC, with the Department of African Affairs of the Ministry of Foreign Affairs as its main sponsor, has also been actively exploring the sustainability of FOCAC.

In the process, they compared and noted the shift between the eight key cooperation objectives agreed in 2006 and those agreed in 2009 (Annex). This can be seen as an important step towards sustainable development.[51] Some Chinese

---

51. Liu Haifang, 'Continuities and transformations: Deep reading of the fourth meeting of FOCAC,' PAMBAZUKA News, December 2009, http://www.pambazuka.org/en/category/africa_china/61089.

Diagram 6: Potential Directions for Decision-making Processes (3)

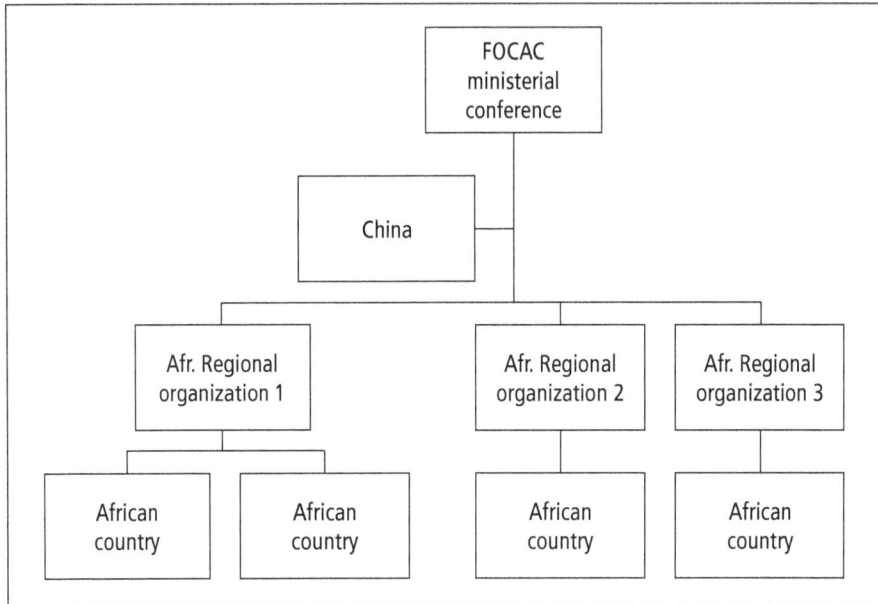

participants hold that there might be disadvantages to the current three-yearly schedule for FOCAC conferences, given Africa's urgent need for livelihood and large-scale infrastructure projects.[52] Improving the process and making it more beneficial to African development is a new decision-making issue for both sides.

The factors outlined above make it very clear that the FOCAC decision-making process is becoming more multivariate and trending towards greater fairness. The attitude of African countries towards FOCAC remains the crucial element in determining these new tendencies, perspectives and directions.

China's attitude will likely remain open to any possibility, and will respect the keenness of Africa in making new initiatives. China seems to look favourably on the emergence of any regional or collective coordination among African countries, which will lighten China's workload (which it has so far solely shouldered) and improve timeliness and work efficiency.[53]

6.4 Reinforcement of Interaction and African Dynamics

There should be greater interaction between China and Africa in the operation of FOCAC. Active engagement by African countries, the AU and related re-

---

52. Interview with Amb. Liu Guijin, 31December 2010, Beijing.
53. Interview with Amb. Liu Guijin, 31December 2010, Beijing.

gional organizations will make FOCAC proposals more relevant to and practical for Africa.

Countries on the continent can coordinate their domestic development plans with FOCAC at the design stage of the agenda. It can be deduced that Africa is not optimising its role in FOCAC as compared to its engagement in the Africa-South America Summit. FOCAC aims to create a win-win situation based on equality and consultation. Therefore African countries should take a more active role in decision-making.

(a) Enhancing the African Union's Functions

Although African countries have different views about AU's role, this cannot impact the AU's involvement in the design of transnational, regional and continental projects, such as regional traffic networks, continental communication networks and water engineering projects. '(The) African Union's role as a mediator of mutual and bilateral interests in FOCAC brings benefits to both China and Africa.'[54] It can set up a standing technocratic office like the Chinese Follow-up Action Committee to cooperate with China, thereby making FOCAC a more professional and scientific organization.

(b) Regional Organizations in Africa Can Contribute More

Regional organizations in Africa, including the Southern African Development Community and Economic Community of West African States, have witnessed rapid development and have recently played a major role in African integration. These organizations can submit more proposals for cooperation opportunities in China-Africa relations. China and Africa could negotiate in a multilateral framework and implement policies and programmes bilaterally. Regional organizations from Africa should take greater advantage of FOCAC and consult more with China.

(c) Institutional Strengthening

China and African countries can promote their collaboration in developing legal systems, anti-corruption measures, market management and financial supervision. At present, there are problems and difficulties within FOCAC related to legal systems and governance capacity. China and Africa can strengthen their cooperation in promoting good governance and capacity building to make their relationship more effective.

---

54. Francis Ikome, 'The role and place of the African Union in the emerging China-Afric partnership,' p.210.

6.5 Improving the Organization and Management of International Cooperation

In China, international cooperation includes foreign aid. Although China's foreign assistance is not specifically included in this research project, these issues were explored in the research process.

(a) China and Foreign Aid

With the change in its status from aid recipient to aid provider, China views international cooperation as one of its important missions as a responsible nation of the world. At present, China's total economic activity is growing rapidly and it constantly increases its aid to other countries. However, the system of foreign assistance has existed for decades without timely adjustment. It is necessary to centralize the management of foreign assistance.

First, a coordinating committee established at ministerial-level could gradually change into a new institution responsible for foreign assistance under the direct leadership of the State Council. The new institution could be called the Administration of International Cooperation in Development, and be directly affiliated to the State Council.

(b) Speed up Legislation on Foreign Assistance

The government should first enact a State Council ordinance to regulate foreign assistance and then upgrade it to a law on foreign assistance.

The publication of the *China's Foreign Aid* white paper is a milestone in China's pursuit of transparency. Considering that all foreign assistance is derived from taxes, the government, as a responsible leader, must keep its citizens informed and respect their right to know about the issue. It is necessary to establish a consultation institution, think-tank and training mechanism for professionals.

Foreign assistance should be delivered within the context of international cooperation and strengthening multilateral cooperation. It is important to reinforce cooperation with regional and international organizations. The present international aid regime has many shortcomings. China should adhere to its own principles, while providing foreign assistance step by step to different countries or projects, and continue to promote international cooperation. It should be noted that countries like South Africa have established their own foreign assistance agencies, while China's other allies, India, Brazil and other countries have also provided development aid for a long time. These countries have similar perspectives to China's on foreign assistance matters. China should collaborate with these countries to enable emerging countries to achieve greater standing in the international foreign aid regime.

China can also learn from the OECD, which collects a wide range of information from ministries of foreign affairs and commerce, professional bodies in different countries, civil organizations and overseas think tanks. All this information serves as the basis for possible assistance plans and programmes. This wide assembly of information and its efficient processing are key characteristics of mature international institutions and of soft power.

Soft power doesn't derive from investment in public diplomacy or overseas image-building projects by government, but relies on the energy of civil society, with governments playing only a coordinating role.[55] Multilateral cooperation concerning Africa is intended to benefit Africa. There are only three preconditions: China's sovereignty; its leading role in making African people better off; and the agreement of Africa.[56]

6.6 Sustainability as a Strategic Principle for FOCAC

FOCAC should use the opportunities presented by China-Africa cooperation to bring forward a sustainable development agenda. The mechanism could be government funded and implemented and take the form of a foreign investment demonstration fund led by the relevant agency. It would support outgoing enterprises and firms in important fields in attaching greater importance to environmental protection and to environmentally sensitive sectors.

Measures could include the timely introduction of environmental guarantee funding to be paid by the investing enterprises. FOCAC could also increase investment in a growing number of biodiversity projects. It should take up the responsibility of global environmental governance as a development partner of Africa and promote regional environmental governance. China must demonstrate concern for environmental protection and adopt a strategic perspective on social responsibility.

(a) Enhance Scientific Decision-making in FOCAC

Given FOCAC's greater role in promoting trade relations between China and Africa, it should aspire to higher levels of professionalism and institutional development and display greater political will and commitment.

Members of FOCAC's Chinese Follow-up Action Committee are subordinate to the State Council, a reflection of the nationwide system. Since the establishment of FOCAC, the collective participation by the 27 Chinese member institutions in all aspect of its activities, from the initiation and organisation of every conference to the execution of decisions, is a reflection not only of a

---

55. Wang Jisi, 'The transformation of the perspective in the study of China's international strategy,' *China International Strategy Review 2008*, Beijing: World Knowledge Press, pp.1–10.

56. Li Anshan, 'From "how could" to "how should": The possibility of trilateral cooperation, 'http://www.pambazuka.org/en/category/features/74884, 13 July 2011.

work regime, but also of China's political advantages. FOCAC is mainly run by China, although Africa's role is absolutely respected through the principle of equal consultation. Consequently, FOCAC still lacks a solidly diversified, multi-channel and multilateral foundation. Thus, FOCAC-funded projects may lack sustainability.

How to design measures to promote sustainable development is a question to be studied and planned beforehand. In order to promote sustainable development, future studies and coordination are required at an early stage of planning. Only by bringing sustainable development into strategic thinking, can FOCAC play a positive role in long-term sustainable development instead of its being an obstacle to the operation of FOCAC.

(b) Strengthen the role of environmental protection in FOCAC

The Ministry of Environmental Protection should be more involved in analysis and policy-making in relation to industry, agriculture, sanitation and collaborative environmental programmes.

Institutionalized inspection and supervision systems must be established and implemented, such as rewards and penalties for an enterprise's environmental conduct and environmental vetoes in professional organizations. Setting very high environmental standards will hold back Africa's development, so African countries and organizations should devise and implement more Africa-oriented and -based standards. The ministries of environmental protection should work with ministries of commerce to address environmental issues.

One Zimbabwean diplomat points out that Africa is becoming drier as a result of climate change. China and Africa could jointly concentrate on this problem. Currently, clean energy projects are the main focus of environmental cooperation between the two sides. Other areas are infrastructure development, agriculture and mining.[57]

A Congolese diplomat says that China is developing new sustainable green energy, such as solar and wind, to promote rural development. This diplomat expresses the hope that 'China can bring this technology to us and help us protect the environment'.[58]

(c) Continue to Improve the Social Responsibility of the Chinese Enterprises

To date, over 100 China's corporations have joined the Global Compact. China continues to increase its overseas investments. It should issue related codes or

---

57. Interview with a diplomat from Zimbabwe, Beijing, December 2010; interview with Amb. Liu Guijin, Beijing, 31 December 2010.
58. Interview with a diplomat from Congo (Kinshasa), Beijing, 14 December 2010.

directions regarding respect for others' sovereignty to guide Chinese enterprises investing in Africa, particularly in discharging their corporate social responsibility in all aspects. China can also consider other measures to encourage Chinese enterprises to meet their social responsibilities, such as a system of rewards and punishments, providing green loans for market entry, etc.

6.7 Conclusions

China and Africa have come a long way in building FOCAC. While the institutional mechanisms are falling into place, there is still significant room for improvement.

(a) Government Guidance in Investment, Pioneer Enterprises and Multi-lateral Cooperation

In the era of economic globalization, China's companies must 'go out'. The 'two resources, two markets' strategy offers China's state-owned enterprises a great opportunity. The current investment style guided by governments and headed by companies is very important to FOCAC. It is recognized that the Chinese government should increase investment step by step in big and middle-sized exploration projects for African resources.

The use of preferential credit and preferential buyers' credit to encourage Chinese companies to cooperate with African countries in the exploitation of resources has obviously prompted companies to invest in Africa. From 1995 to 1998, total Chinese investments were around $ 3.68 billion, and almost 381 companies were established, including CNPC and Dongfeng Automobile.[59]

The establishment of FOCAC created more opportunities for commercial cooperation with Africa. The 2010 data show that nearly 2,180 Chinese companies expanded into Africa; around 8,000 projects were under way, including projects worth more than $ 1 billion such as power generation stations, ports, airports, freeways and sanitation.[60] For comparison, in 1999 trade between China and Africa was $ 6.48 billion, in 2000 more than $ 10 billion, but by 2010 the figure had reached $ 126.9 billion.[61]

Recently in FOCAC the forum of African and Chinese entrepreneurs has been started. Some African countries have also established special economic zones. All of these efforts have advanced FOCAC and Sino-African relations.

---

59. Chen Gongyuan, *Studies on the History of China-Africa Friendly Relations,* Beijing: Society of China African Studies, October 2010, pp. 147–9.
60. 'Chinese companies increased investments in Africa,' 26 July 2010, http://news.hexun.com/2010-07-26/124359907.html.
61. Speech of Xie Ya-jing, Vice Director of Department of West Asia and Africa of MOFCOM at the lauching ceremony of Research Forum of the Society of African Studies, 27 April 2011.

(b) Active Involvement by and Strong Support of Africa

Researchers interviewed several African ambassadors for this study. They have very positive attitudes towards FOCAC and especially emphasized the importance of the principles it enshrines, including equality, programme feasibility and mutual benefit.

Ambassadors from Tunisia, the Democratic Republic of the Congo, Morocco, Zimbabwe, Nigeria and the Sudan acknowledged that Chinese and African interactions through FOCAC have further promoted China-Africa relations and cooperation. They emphasized three aspects: the equal relations in FOCAC, the positive role with regard to development; and the concrete character of projects. The Sudanese diplomat remarked that FOCAC is established on the basis of equal bilateral relations,[62] while the Tunisian ambassador said that the African continental economy had grown by 6 per cent in the past 10 years, one third of which (2 per cent) should be attributed to China. FOCAC has become a framework for choosing the best means to define African needs, project priorities and common goals. A significant feature of FOCAC policy is its pragmatism and focus in deciding on areas of concrete cooperation, priorities in implementing projects and in marshalling resources to solve problems.

FOCAC policies are targeted to Africa's practical needs and urgent issues and to resolving problems to the benefit of African development.[63] The DRC diplomat noted that Africa and, in particular, the DRC appreciate what China has promised African partners, 'because China has brought about a new model of cooperation', which is both unprecedented and truly fruitful. China-Africa cooperation has brought change throughout Africa, especially in infrastructure.[64]

FOCAC is a form of South-South cooperation. All members are developing countries, and they are equal. This point was made by the Moroccan ambassador, who highlighted FOCAC's great achievements over the past 10 years. It differs from other forums in its pragmatism and fact-based approach. FOCAC has covered many fields and especially the sustainability projects would contribute a great deal to African development.[65]

A Zimbabwean diplomat reported that Zimbabwe had greatly benefited from FOCAC in the fields of agriculture, the service sector and infrastructure. He considered the relationship equal, with China and Africa sitting together within the framework to discuss major issues. Although China is economically very strong, Africa can still play an important role in FOCAC.[66] A Nigerian diplomat expressed his satisfaction towards FOCAC for its support of sustainable

---

62. Interview with a diplomat from the Sudan, Beijing, 2 December 2010.
63. Interview with Tunisian ambassador, Beijing, 7 December 2010.
64. Interview with a diplomat from DRC, Beijing, 14 December 2010.
65. Interview with Moroccan ambassador, Beijing, 10 December 2010.
66. Interview with Zimbabwe ambassador, Beijing, 14 December 2010.

development and its support for several aspects of the Nigerian government's development agenda. Consequently, Nigeria sees cooperation through FOCAC as gradually increasing Nigerian power and believes that China-Africa relations will benefit both parties in the long term. FOCAC plays an indispensable role in China-Africa relations and has become a celebrated model of multilateral international cooperation.[67]

Promoting African development is the objective of China-Africa cooperation. China's own experience of development shows that no country can develop by depending on aid. Its cooperation with Africa is based on this experience, particularly that development relies more on investment and trade. Of course, China has a flexible policy towards Africa countries. For countries lacking in resources and markets, there will be more assistance, but for countries rich in both, there will be more international trade and investment.

---

67. Interview with a diplomat from Nigeria, Beijing, 30 December 2010.

ANNEX

Follow-up Action Achieved

First Ministerial Conference
Political relations, regional peace and security
- Chinese leaders visited Africa 20 times, more than 30 African top leaders visited China
- Supported set-up of AU and implementation of NEPAD;
- Sent peacekeeping forces to UN in DRC and Liberia in 2003.

Economic relations
- Signed Bilateral Investment Protection Treaty with more than 20 African countries;
- Established Centres for the Promotion of Chinese Investment and Trade in 11 countries;
- Set up 117 new enterprises in Africa;
- The volume of trade was US$ 18.545 billion in 2003, increased 49.7% compared to the previous year and up 75% from 2000.

Social Development
- Signed 245 new economic-assistance agreements;
- Exempted 156 items of debt of 31 African countries, totaling RMB 10.5 billion;
- Set up AHRDF, trained 6,000 professionals, sent 500 specialists to Africa;
- Medical aid agreements with 40 African countries;
- Cooperated in preventing and treating AIDS, malaria and pulmonary tuberculosis;
- Organized the event of 'Environmental Protection in China for Africa' on October 23, 2003 in Beijing.

Cultural exchanges and cooperation
- Egypt, South Africa, and Morocco became the Approved Destination Status for Chinese citizens traveling abroad.

Second Ministerial Conference
Political relations, regional peace and security
- 34 African presidents, prime ministers and vice presidents visited China;
- Sent 435 Chinese to Sudan to support UN peacekeeping in May 2006;
- Sent 1,273 peacekeeping personnel to Africa and took part in 7 peacekeeping actions led by the UN.

Economic relations
- Chinese direct investments in Africa totaled US$ 1.595 billion at the end of 2005;
- In 2005, bilateral trade volume reached $ 39.8 billion, an increase of 34.9 % compared to 2004;
- 190 commodities from 28 African LDCs fell under the tariff-free policy.

Social Development
- Set up the Inter-departmental Coordinating Mechanism of Foreign Human Resources Development and Cooperation;
- Train 7,600 Africans; sent several hundred experts to Africa;
- Held the conference on China-Africa environmental cooperation in Nairobi on 21 February 2005;
- Published China's African Policy Paper on 12 January 2006.

Cultural exchanges and cooperation
- Start to send Chinese volunteers to Africa;
- 'Meeting in Beijing' and the 'Voyage of Chinese Culture to Africa' held in 2004 and 2006;
- 17 African countries became destinations for Chinese tourists.

Beijing Summit and Third Ministerial Conference
Political relations, regional peace and security
- High officials visited 36 African countries; 36 African presidents, vice presidents, prime ministers and Speakers visited China;
- Started China-AU strategic dialogue, plus two further rounds of dialogue; support the construction of the AU conference centre;
- Deployed 6,281 peacekeepers and police to Africa; deployed 4 naval ships for escort duty in the Gulf of Aden off Somalia; helped protect more than 100 ships.

Economic relations
- Established bilateral mixed economic and trade commission with 4 African countries;
- Total number of mutual investment protection agreements was 31;
- China-Africa Development Fund set up, invest more than $ 500 million in 27 projects;
- Constructed six Chinese SEZ;
- Trade reaches US$ 106.8 billion in 2008;
- 478 commodities from 31 African LDCs enjoyed the tariff-free policy;
- More than 10 bilateral agricultural cooperation agreements with African countries;
- Send 100 senior agricultural experts to and set up 10 agricultural centres in Africa.

Social Development
- Doubled assistance by the end of 2009 from 2006; provided US$ 2.647 billion in preferential loans to support 54 projects in 28 African countries and US$ 2 billion in preferential export buyer's credits to support 11 projects in 10 African countries;
- Cancelled debts owed by the 33 HIDCs;
- Trained 15,000 African professionals;
- Built 96 rural schools in Africa;
- Provide teaching equipment for 30 schools;
- Sponsorship for African students increased to 4,000; open 23 Confucius Institutes or classrooms in 16 African countries;
- Built 28 hospitals in African countries; build 30 malaria prevention and treatment centres in Africa;
- Sent 1,200 Chinese medical workers to 42 African countries and regions.

Cultural exchanges and cooperation
- 15 African cultural delegations visited China; 20 Chinese artist groups visited Africa;
- Dispatched 281 youth volunteers to Africa;
- All China Women's Federation sets up five women's training and exchange centres in Africa and provides 28 batches of material assistance to women's organizations in 14 African countries;
- 9 African countries become destinations for Chinese tourist groups

Fourth Ministerial Conference
Political relations, regional peace and security
- The first 'FOCAC – Law Forum' in Cairo in 2009, more than 80 legal experts from China and over 20 African and West-Asian countries attended;
- Bilateral high-lever visits from both side;
- Party-to-party exchanges on administration experience;
- AU building finished and AU becomes member of FOCAC.

Economic relations
- 33 mutual investment protection agreements reached;
- Signed the Avoidance of Double Taxation Agreement with 11 African countries;

- The volume of trade was $ 126.9 billion in 2010;
- Over 4,700 items covering 95% of commodities from Africa enjoyed tariff-free policy;
- Held China-Africa Agriculture Cooperation Forum in 2010;
- Launched the China- Africa Science and Technology Partner Programme and the Ceremony of Equipment Donated to African Researchers in 2009.

Social Development

- Hosted the Eighth Meeting of the Foreign Aid in Education in Developing Countries and the launching ceremony of China-Africa Cooperation Programme of Universities 20 +20 in Guangzhou, 2 June 2010;
- Published the China-Africa Economic and Trade Cooperation in 2010;
- Built 100 clean energy projects.

Cultural exchanges and cooperation

- 'African Culture in Focus 2010' was hosted in China;
- Launched the China-Africa Joint Research and Exchange Program in Beijing on 30 March 2010.

For more details, please refer to the website of the Ministry of Foreign Affairs, People's Republic of China: http://www.focac.org/eng/.

DISCUSSION PAPERS PUBLISHED BY THE INSTITUTE

Recent issues in the series are available electronically for download free of charge
www.nai.uu.se

1. Kenneth Hermele and Bertil Odén, *Sanctions and Dilemmas. Some Implications of Economic Sanctions against South Africa.*
1988. 43 pp. ISBN 91-7106-286-6

2. Elling Njål Tjønneland, *Pax Pretoriana. The Fall of Apartheid and the Politics of Regional Destabilisation.*
1989. 31 pp. ISBN 91-7106-292-0

3. Hans Gustafsson, Bertil Odén and Andreas Tegen, *South African Minerals. An Analysis of Western Dependence.*
1990. 47 pp. ISBN 91-7106-307-2

4. Bertil Egerö, *South African Bantustans. From Dumping Grounds to Battlefronts.*
1991. 46 pp. ISBN 91-7106-315-3

5. Carlos Lopes, *Enough is Enough! For an Alternative Diagnosis of the African Crisis.*
1994. 38 pp. ISBN 91-7106-347-1

6. Annika Dahlberg, *Contesting Views and Changing Paradigms.*
1994. 59 pp. ISBN 91-7106-357-9

7. Bertil Odén, *Southern African Futures. Critical Factors for Regional Development in Southern Africa.*
1996. 35 pp. ISBN 91-7106-392-7

8. Colin Leys and Mahmood Mamdani, *Crisis and Reconstruction – African Perspectives.*
1997. 26 pp. ISBN 91-7106-417-6

9. Gudrun Dahl, *Responsibility and Partnership in Swedish Aid Discourse.*
2001. 30 pp. ISBN 91-7106-473-7

10. Henning Melber and Christopher Saunders, *Transition in Southern Africa – Comparative Aspects.*
2001. 28 pp. ISBN 91-7106-480-X

11. *Regionalism and Regional Integration in Africa.*
2001. 74 pp. ISBN 91-7106-484-2

12. Souleymane Bachir Diagne, et al., *Identity and Beyond: Rethinking Africanity.*
2001. 33 pp. ISBN 91-7106-487-7

13. Georges Nzongola-Ntalaja, et al., *Africa in the New Millennium.* Edited by Raymond Suttner.
2001. 53 pp. ISBN 91-7106-488-5

14. *Zimbabwe's Presidential Elections 2002.* Edited by Henning Melber.
2002. 88 pp. ISBN 91-7106-490-7

15. Birgit Brock-Utne, *Language, Education and Democracy in Africa.*
2002. 47 pp. ISBN 91-7106-491-5

16. Henning Melber et al., *The New Partnership for Africa's development (NEPAD).*
2002. 36 pp. ISBN 91-7106-492-3

17. Juma Okuku, *Ethnicity, State Power and the Democratisation Process in Uganda.*
2002. 42 pp. ISBN 91-7106-493-1

18. Yul Derek Davids, et al., *Measuring Democracy and Human Rights in Southern Africa.* Compiled by Henning Melber.
2002. 50 pp. ISBN 91-7106-497-4

19. Michael Neocosmos, Raymond Suttner and Ian Taylor, *Political Cultures in Democratic South Africa.* Compiled by Henning Melber.
2002. 52 pp. ISBN 91-7106-498-2

20. Martin Legassick, *Armed Struggle and Democracy. The Case of South Africa.*
2002. 53 pp. ISBN 91-7106-504-0

21. Reinhart Kössler, Henning Melber and Per Strand, *Development from Below. A Namibian Case Study.*
2003. 32 pp. ISBN 91-7106-507-5

22. Fred Hendricks, *Fault-Lines in South African Democracy. Continuing Crises of Inequality and Injustice.*
2003. 32 pp. ISBN 91-7106-508-3

23. Kenneth Good, *Bushmen and Diamonds. (Un) Civil Society in Botswana.*
2003. 39 pp. ISBN 91-7106-520-2

24. Robert Kappel, Andreas Mehler, Henning Melber and Anders Danielson, *Structural Stability in an African Context.*
2003. 55 pp. ISBN 91-7106-521-0

25. Patrick Bond, *South Africa and Global Apartheid. Continental and International Policies and Politics.*
2004. 45 pp. ISBN 91-7106-523-7

26. Bonnie Campbell (ed.), *Regulating Mining in Africa. For whose benefit?*
2004. 89 pp. ISBN 91-7106-527-X

27. Suzanne Dansereau and Mario Zamponi, *Zimbabwe – The Political Economy of Decline.* Compiled by Henning Melber.
2005. 43 pp. ISBN 91-7106-541-5

28. Lars Buur and Helene Maria Kyed, *State Recognition of Traditional Authority in Mozambique. The nexus of Community Representation and State Assist-ance.* 2005. 30 pp. ISBN 91-7106-547-4

29. Hans Eriksson and Björn Hagströmer, *Chad – Towards Democratisation or Petro-Dictatorship?* 2005. 82 pp.ISBN 91-7106-549-

30. Mai Palmberg and Ranka Primorac (eds), *Skinning the Skunk – Facing Zimbabwean Futures.* 2005. 40 pp. ISBN 91-7106-552-0

31. Michael Brüntrup, Henning Melber and Ian Taylor, *Africa, Regional Cooperation and the World Market – Socio-Economic Strategies in Times of Global Trade Regimes.* Com-piled by Henning Melber. 2006. 70 pp. ISBN 91-7106-559-8

32. Fibian Kavulani Lukalo, *Extended Handshake or Wrestling Match? – Youth and Urban Culture Celebrating Politics in Kenya.* 2006.58 pp. ISBN 91-7106-567-9

33. Tekeste Negash, *Education in Ethiopia: From Crisis to the Brink of Collapse.* 2006. 55 pp. ISBN 91-7106-576-8

34. Fredrik Söderbaum and Ian Taylor (eds) *Micro-Regionalism in West Africa. Evidence from Two Case Studies.* 2006. 32 pp. ISBN 91-7106-584-9

35. Henning Melber (ed.), *On Africa – Scholars and African Studies.* 2006. 68 pp. ISBN 978-91-7106-585-8

36. Amadu Sesay, *Does One Size Fit All? The Sierra Leone Truth and Reconciliation Commission Revisited.* 2007. 56 pp. ISBN 978-91-7106-586-5

37. Karolina Hulterström, Amin Y. Kamete and Henning Melber, *Political Opposition in African Countries – The Case of Kenya, Namibia, Zambia and Zimbabwe.* 2007. 86 pp. ISBN 978-7106-587-2

38. Henning Melber (ed.), *Governance and State Delivery in Southern Africa. Examples from Botswana, Namibia and Zimbabwe.* 2007. 65 pp. ISBN 978-91-7106-587-2

39. Cyril Obi (ed.), *Perspectives on Côte d'Ivoire: Between Political Breakdown and Post-Conflict Peace.* 2007. 66 pp. ISBN 978-91-7106-606-6

40. Anna Chitando, *Imagining a Peaceful Society. A Vision of Children's Literature in a Post-Conflict Zimbabwe.* 2008. 26 pp. ISBN 978-91-7106-623-7

41. Olawale Ismail, *The Dynamics of Post-Conflict Reconstruction and Peace Building in West Africa. Between Change and Stability.* 2009.52 pp. ISBN 978-91-7106-637-4

42. Ron Sandrey and Hannah Edinger, *Examining the South Africa–China Agricultural Relationship.* 2009. 58 pp. ISBN 978-91-7106-643-5

43. Xuan Gao, *The Proliferation of Anti-Dumping and Poor Governance in Emerging Economies.* 2009. 41 pp. ISBN 978-91-7106-644-2

44. Lawal Mohammed Marafa, *Africa's Business and Development Relationship with China. Seeking Moral and Capital Values of the Last Economic Frontier.* 2009. xx pp. ISBN 978-91-7106-645-9

45. Mwangi wa Githinji, *Is That a Dragon or an Elephant on Your Ladder? The Potential Impact of China and India on Export Led Growth in African Countries.* 2009. 40 pp. ISBN 978-91-7106-646-6

46. Jo-Ansie van Wyk, *Cadres, Capitalists, Elites and Coalitions. The ANC, Business and Development in South Africa.* 2009. 61 pp. ISBN 978-91-7106-656-5

47. Elias Courson, *Movement for the Emancipation of the Niger Delta (MEND). Political Marginalization, Repression and Petro-Insurgency in the Niger Delta.*2009. 30 pp. ISBN 978-91-7106-657-2

48. Babatunde Ahonsi, *Gender Violence and HIV/AIDS in Post-Conflict West Africa. Issues and Responses.* 2010. 38 pp. ISBN 978-91-7106-665-7

49. Usman Tar and Abba Gana Shettima, *Endangered Democracy? The Struggle over Secularism and its Implications for Politics and Democracy in Nigeria.* 2010. 21 pp. ISBN 978-91-7106-666-4

50. Garth Andrew Myers, *Seven Themes in African Urban Dynamics.*2010. 28 pp. ISBN 978-91-7106-677-0

51. Abdoumaliq Simone, *The Social Infrastructures of City Life in Contemporary Africa.* 2010. 33 pp. ISBN 978-91-7106-678-7

52. Li Anshan, *Chinese Medical Cooperation in Africa. With Special Emphasis on the Medical Teams and Anti-Malaria Campaign.* 2011. 24 pp. ISBN 978-91-7106-683-1

53. Folashade Hunsu, *Zangbeto: Navigating the Spaces Between Oral art, Communal Security And Conflict Mediation in Badagry, Nigeria.* 2011. 27 pp. ISBN 978-91-7106-688-6

54. Jeremiah O. Arowosegbe, *Reflections on the Challenge of Reconstructing Post-Conflict States in West Africa: Insights from Claude Ake's Political Writings.*
2011. 40 pp. ISBN 978-91-7106-689-3

55. Bertil Odén, *The Africa Policies of Nordic Countries and the Erosion of the Nordic Aid Model: A comparative study.*
2011. 66 pp. ISBN 978-91-7106-691-6

56. Angela Meyer, P*eace and Security Cooperation in Central Africa: Developments, Challenges and Prospects.*
2011. 47 pp ISBN 978-91-7106-693-0

57. Godwin R. Murunga, *Spontaneous or Premeditated? Post-Election Violence in Kenya.*
2011. 58 pp. ISBN 978-91-7106-694-7

58. David Sebudubudu & Patrick Molutsi, *The Elite as a Critical Factor in National Development: The Case of Botswana.*
2011. 48 pp. ISBN 978-91-7106-695-4

59. Sabelo J. Ndlovu-Gatsheni, *The Zimbabwean Nation-State Project. A Historical Diagnosis of Identity and Power-Based Conflicts in a Postcolonial State.*
2011. 97 pp. ISBN 978-91-7106-696-1

60. Jide Okeke, *Why Humanitarian Aid in Darfur is not a Practice of the 'Responsibility to Protect'.*
2011. 45 pp. ISBN 978-91-7106-697-8

62. Osita A. Agbu, *Ethnicity and Democratisation in Africa. Challenges for Politics and Development.*
2011, 30 pp. ISBN 978-91-7106-699-2

63. Cheryl Hendricks, *Gender and Security in Africa. An Overview.*
2011, 32 pp. ISBN 978-91-7106-700-5

64. Adebayo O. Olukoshi, *Democratic Governance and Accountability in Africa. In Search of a Workable Framework.*
2011, 25 pp. ISBN 978-91-7106-701-2

65. Christian Lund, *Land Rights and Citizenship in Africa.*
2011, 31 pp. ISBN 978-91-7106-705-0

66. Lars Rudebeck, *Electoral Democratisation in Post-Civil War Guinea-Bissau 1999–2008.*
2011, 31 pp. ISBN 978-91-7106-706-7

67. Kidane Mengisteab, *Critical Factors in the Horn of Africa's Raging Conflicts.*
2011, 39 pp. ISBN 978-91-7106-707-4

68. Solomon T. Ebobrah, *Reconceptualising Democratic Local Governance in the Niger Delta.*
2011, 32 pp. ISBN 978-91-7106-709-8

69. Linda Darkwa, *The Challenge of Sub-regional Security in West Africa. The Case of the 2006 Ecowas Convention on Small Arms and Light Weapons.*
2011, 39 pp. ISBN 978-91-7106-710-4

70. J.Shola Omotola, *Unconstitutional Changes of Government in Africa. What Implications for Democratic Consolidation?*
2011, 49 pp. ISBN 978-91-7106-711-4

71. Wale Adebanwi, *Globally Oriented Citizenship and International Voluntary Service. Interrogating Nigeria's Technical Aid Corps Scheme.*
2011, 81 pp. ISBN 978-91-7106-713-5

72. Göran Holmqvist, *Inequality and Identity. Causes of War?*
2012, 42 pp. ISBN 978-91-7106-714-2

73. Ike Okonta, *Biafran Ghosts. The MASSOB Ethnic Militia and Nigeria's Democratisation Process.*
2012, 64 pp. ISBN 978-91-7106-716-6

74. Li Anshan, Liu Haifang,Pan Huaqiong, Zeng Aiping and He Wenping, *FOCAC Twelve Years Later. Achievements, Challenges and the Way Forward.*
2012, 63 pp. ISBN 978-91-7106-718-0

www.ingramcontent.com/pod-product-compliance
Lightning Source LLC
Chambersburg PA
CBHW080209300326
41934CB00039B/3426